GODDESSES FART TOO

A modern guide to spiritual enlightenment for increased happiness, patience, and inner peace

CRYSTAL GRAY

D0188297

preface

Hi! I'm Crystal.

I'm a lot of things—a mom, wife, daughter, sister, organic vegetable farmer, yogi, spiritual seeker, and lover of good food, animals, and life. I want to begin by saying that I'm not an expert on anything.

Well, maybe on fucking up, but that's about it.

I'm a yoga teacher, yes, but there will always be more to learn. I'm definitely not a perfect yogi and will never claim to be.

Writing this book became a journey into my soul, into helping me uncover who I am, under all the labels I've given to myself over this lifetime.

I hope that it can help you do the same. It's important to figure out who you are underneath everything because that is the only part that is real and the only part that will remain long after your physical body is gone.

I must warn you, if you keep reading, you'll learn about some of the dark and desperate places I've been in my life.

It wasn't my dream to share these things with the world, especially when so many of us will do anything to hide those secrets. However, this is part of my healing process and, in turn, I hope it helps you heal by making you realize you ARE worthy, no matter where you've been.

You *do* matter and you do have something important to share with the world, no matter how big or small (that's all a matter of perspective anyway).

Before you go on, you may want to ask yourself what you are looking for in your life at this time. This will be your guiding force as you make your way through this book.

Are you looking for . . .
- Clarity
- A sense of purpose
- Spiritual growth
- Healing
- Support
- Self-love
- A feeling that you're not alone
- Faith

Did any of these ring true? Now would be a great time to journal and start this journey with direction so you can get the most out of it.

CHAPTER 1

My mistrust of women

As I write this, I am returning from a week-long retreat I was leading in Costa Rica with my soul sisters.

A few different Goddesses came and shared their knowledge with the group. Every single one of the people that came were exactly the people that were supposed to be there. You could just tell. There were signs.

Signs, for me, usually show up as synchronicities. There were just too many of these similarities on this trip to overlook or disregard. We each had a connection that was almost unbelievable.

Some of the more amazing ones were that one of the girls and I share a birthday. One of the girls' maternal grandfather died in the same uncommon way as my dad. The owner's brother, who is also a yoga teacher, named his daughter, who is one year older than my daughter, Aya, the *same* name as my daughter. Then I found out one of the girls in the group was born in the same city as I was and we have both lived in other states for years.

I'm mentioning this because, all too often, we can overlook things, and if we would just PAY ATTENTION, we could open ourselves up to receive SO. MUCH. MORE.

One of the things that has made the biggest impact in my life and in how I am able to open myself up to Divine Guidance is *sisterhood.*

Putting myself out there over the past couple of years, sharing my knowledge while not claiming to have all the answers and instead, being open to learning new ideas while supporting, encouraging, and lifting up other women.

During this yoga retreat, I laughed more than I probably ever have in my life. We cried, we danced, we held each other in sacred space. It was life-changing.

You might think, well, that's all fine and good, but I don't have girlfriends or the friends I do have aren't into this kind of stuff.

I hear you.

Growing up, I had two older brothers, and I was definitely a tomboy. During high school, I was always one of the guys and found it so much easier to be around them than around girls.

I always felt like I had to dim my light around other women and could never be who I truly was because I might make them jealous, or they might not like me because I was too . . . me.

When I moved from my small hometown to a slightly bigger town during my freshman year, I was not welcomed warmly--at least not by the girls. I was called a slut (even though I didn't have sex until I was 18) and fat. Those are the ones that stuck with me the most. Any time I did act like I liked myself at all, I was labeled as self-absorbed or stuck up.

That's where my trust issues with women began, and 20 years later, I'm finally getting over it. It's taken a lot of work, a lot of listening to my Intuition and a lot of help from my angels, guides, and the law of attraction to bring some incredible women into my circle.

You'll see that as you start to shift your life, the people around you will shift, too. Some you'll lose touch with and some will just not be around as much anymore.

This may be sad or hard to deal with at first, but as you grow, you need to make room for the new to come in--and that includes your new tribe.

These women will have your back.

These women won't judge you because they know they have baggage, too.

These women will open up and SHARE their baggage with you, not act like their shit doesn't stink.

These women will listen to your stories and laugh their asses off instead of acting like you're fucking nuts.

I wasn't expecting to receive as much as these women who came along on the retreat because I was focused on giving. I couldn't have imagined that the growth I experienced would spark the start of this book.

And it all started with a Really. Loud. Fart.

CHAPTER 2

My Aha Moment

I know what you're thinking: How can a spiritual woman say her "aha" moment was because of a fart? Well, I'm about to tell you, so don't get your panties in a bunch.

It all started on our second to last night of the retreat. We had gotten really close and had shared a lot.

After dinner, on our way back up to our rooms, my good friend, Suzanne, and I started heading up our path while the ladies rooming in the other house started up their path--which was about 20 feet or so from ours.

It was then that I decided it would be really, really funny to rip a huge fart. I wasn't sure if it would even be a good one, but . . . it was.

The girls on the other path stopped and looked our way, expecting to see a large animal of some sort scurrying across the ground making farting noises, so they were very surprised when we told them what the noise really was!

When they started laughing their asses off, doubling over, and almost peeing their pants, I KNEW this was my crew. I also knew that if I can make more people laugh like this, it's definitely something I want to do more of!

(Wait for it, it gets better. Promise!)

The next day, some of us were down by the beach and Suzanne brought up another hilarious story.

One, like a lot of others, that I had only shared with her because, well, there are things in your head that you just REALLY want to know if other people feel the same but you can't ask just ANYone because they'll think you're really out of your mind.

I decided to share the story with these other Goddesses, and sure enough, we all laughed until tears were streaming down our faces. I was on to something.

For years, I had been trying to figure out how to be more ME, how to share more of me. And on this trip, I realized that I CAN be both spiritual--a Goddess, while also being a woman who likes to do really vulgar things to get a laugh. It's something I love most in the world.

And to know that these sisters with me thought it was just as funny as I did, well, then I knew there had to be more out there-- maybe you're one of them and maybe you're not.

Either way is OK.

It's time to stop thinking about what version of yourself you want to share with the world. Especially when it comes to social media. It's so easy to come up with an image and only show THAT to the world. The reality is that the world doesn't want to see your polished, perfect self (the one that doesn't exist), it yearns to see the *real* you. Once you start stepping into your fears, so that you can grow like you know you need to, you'll begin impacting the world in ways you never thought possible.

Why?

Because you are the only person that can do *you*. The only one on this whole planet that can shine your unique light because of everything you've learned over this lifetime and all the other ones, too.

Isn't that liberating?

It's time to rise up and start being unapologetically you. The YOU you came here to be. Now, it might not be someone who farts in front of other people, but I share that story because of the real reason why I do it.

Well, one: because I love making people laugh, already said that, but the main reason is that when I am able to say F*ck it and just let loose and not apologize for who I really am and how I really act, it paves the way for others around me to do the same.

They might feel more confident to speak their truth, to open up, and share their story. Or being a little bit more *them*.

This is the true gift. This is the magic. THIS is the lesson.

You can be a Goddess, no matter what type of woman you are. You don't have to be skinny, you don't have to have perfect hair, you don't have to wear certain clothes or go to yoga six times per week.

But you *can* be *you*. Farts, cuss words, and all.

Be your own brand of Goddess--not mine or anyone else's. That's what the world needs and that's what I teach in my yoga teacher training classes and yoga business mentoring.

The world doesn't need any more of whoever your teacher is or whoever is already "making it" in the business you are trying to make it in.

They'll always be better at being them, but guess what? You'll ALWAYS be best at being you.

Start figuring out who in the F that person is--*really* is.

You are a Goddess because you are you. In fact, the more you can step into that--the parts you think are ugly and dark and shameful as well as the parts of you that are shiny, clean and polished--the more likely it is you will reach your full potential because not only will you get to live your purpose, you'll inspire countless others to do the same.

That's what's going to change the world.

JOURNALING PROMPT:

- What type of Goddess are you?
- What parts of you make you feel like you're not good enough to be a Goddess?
- Is it true?
- Why or why not?
- How can you look those feelings in the eye and uncover those shadows?

CHAPTER 3

*Goddesses F*ck Up, Too*

I remember sitting in church as a little girl, listening to the minister give his sermon, and thinking, "There has to be more to this stuff that no one is telling us." As soon as I got old enough and learned there were other religions, I started looking into many of them, trying to find my place. I soon realized that none of them answered all of my questions, so I never really felt like I found my spiritual home.

Then I found yoga.

When I started doing yoga, I realized that everything I had been searching for outside of myself was actually within me all along.

This was a huge turning point in my life and one that helped me slowly overcome addictions and other issues. For years, I had tried to get back to that spiritual place that I, somewhere, deep down, remembered. I used alcohol and drugs to get there because it was the only way I knew to alter my state of mind and tap in to different ways of being.

I almost died--a few times--trying to get there.

My drinking began in high school and just increased from there. The more I realized I didn't know what I wanted to do with my life, the more I wanted to escape the fact that I didn't have a path. Everyone always puts so much pressure on young people to have a plan and have direction. There are so many requirements on how to do that, but they usually don't require listening to your heart.

This is a major mistake.

We are put here on this planet to do something that is our gift from God. This purpose or way we share this purpose with the world may change at different times in our lives but it doesn't matter if you can "make a good living" by doing it or not. I've found, over the years, that if you are passionate about something enough, you will be always divinely supported and your needs will be met as long as you believe that to be so.

To push a young person into a career because it "makes sense," is socially acceptable, or will make a lot of money, is telling them to turn off that connection they have to their Intuition and their inner knowing. There are many times in childhood when this happens but this one can cause the most grief because it can set them up for a lifetime of being stuck doing something that doesn't fulfill them.

I'm lucky, I was able to follow my dreams, but because I didn't know what I really, really wanted to do, and why I was really here, I floundered and my self-worth was in the gutter.

When I moved to Los Angeles to study fashion merchandising after studying the same thing, near my family, I quickly fell into the "rock star lifestyle" and went down a rabbit hole that I can only say a miracle got me out of before it was too late.

I started out drinking and dabbling with drugs, settling on a steady diet of alcohol and cocaine which, after a few months, turned into alcohol and crystal meth. My weight dwindled from a healthy 130 pounds down to a very unhealthy 110 pounds, which, on my 5'5" frame did not a good look make.

I finally pulled myself out of it because of a couple wake-up calls. The first one came when my entire apartment complex evacuated after the fire alarms went off and firemen came in, banged on everyone's doors, and got everyone out.

Except me. I never woke up.

I had been on a couple-day bender and my body was so extremely undernourished and exhausted--most likely near death from the amount of drugs I'd ingested--I slept through the entire thing. Obviously, I'm still alive today so the building didn't end up burning down, but God, my angels or some other being watching my ass was sure as hell with me that day.

I realized my job on Earth was not done. Problem was, I still didn't know what it was!

Not long after that incident, my mom told me that she was going to cut me off if I didn't come home. Since I wouldn't have any money to pay rent, support my habit, or buy the one taco a day that I had been living on, I had no choice but to move home or move in with a guy who'd happily support my habit in exchange for being his girlfriend, I pulled up my big girl pants and made the best decision I've ever made, which was to move back home.

It took me a few months to recover, heal my body, and get my energy back but I did it with the help and support of my family.

I was ashamed and carry a lot of guilt about this with me today, but I know I wouldn't be the woman I am now had that experience not happened.

I realized that I want to be someone who won't ever cast anyone away because of mistakes they think they've made. I want to be a beacon for souls who feel helpless or feel like their lives are meaningless.

Every. One. Matters.

And *everyone* makes mistakes. We are spirits having a *human* experience. If we just supported each other more, made fewer judgments, forgave and took things a little less seriously--this *is*, after all, not our first lifetime, and most likely, not even one of our first 100 lifetimes, so, in the grand scheme of things, all these things we make out to be such huge deals really aren't after all.

Throughout this book, you will find ways to:

- Start cutting yourself some slack.
- Learn to listen and trust your Intuition.
- Stop feeling lost, helpless, hopeless, stuck, and alone.
- Be more authentic, more you.
- Love yourself more.
- Accept yourself more, *all* the parts of you.
- Enjoy the gift that is this lifetime. You'll never have this

one again.

- Find a tribe.
- Start living like you freaking mean it.
- Gain courage to live your dreams.
- Laugh.

Looking for Signs

Signs are a way that the unseen Universe can communicate with you. Be it angels, spirit guides, ancestors--you name it, they'll use signs to help guide you on your path. The key is to start opening yourself up to receive, or rather, notice when the signs appear.

One of the biggest signs I've ever received was at a time when I lived in Los Angeles. As mentioned earlier, these were some dark-ass times. I used to regret this time in my life, but I now can see how everything has woven together perfectly to get me where I am today.

This sign came when it was time for me to make a decision in my life. It was a HUGE turning point and shaped the course of my life forever.

One afternoon, I awoke from a much-needed night's sleep after days of being on drugs, to the sound of wings flapping and scratching on the window. I was startled, but more so confused, when I realized what was making these sounds.

All the screens were perfectly fine in all my windows, there were no holes in my walls or any way for anything to get in besides the door, and yet there was a pigeon--or a dove, I'm not sure--sitting *in* my apartment. I was stunned and just wanted to get that thing out of my apartment without hurting myself, or it, in the process.

Needless to say, I was shaken up. It was one of those things that happen so fast and is so surreal at the same time that after it's done you wonder if it really happened at all! But I knew it did. I was perfectly sober at that time and knew there was no explanation other than it was a huge fucking wake up call, and I needed to listen or shit was going to get real bad, real quick.

I had already been thinking that I needed to make some decisions about my life. My mom told me that she was cutting me off if I didn't come home, and since I had no skills at that point and couldn't pass a drug test, I could either go home and get better or I could stay and try to score drugs however I could.

Thank you, God, that I chose the latter. At that point, I seriously considered both options.

It's unbelievable to me now but that's the state I was in. I couldn't imagine my life without drugs and didn't know how I'd ever be able to have fun or be happy again. Not long after that incident, I moved home.

JOURNALING PROMPT:

- What signs is the Universe giving you that you've already started to catch a glimpse of?
- Have you ever been through a horrible experience that might have actually been a teachable moment?
- What moments made you stronger? More powerful? What signs can you see as a result?

The Road to Recovery

Now, this has been a long road. I'd say I'm still in recovery now because it's always something that I have to deal with. I may not think about doing drugs anymore but sometimes checking out and spending the day drinking with my friends sounds more enticing than working all day on my business.

I can happily say that I almost always choose not to check out anymore, and when I do, it's usually in healthy ways such as meditation or yoga. These are things that give me an escape while helping me tune into who I really am.

When I moved home from Los Angeles, I was a hot mess. I had been using drugs almost daily for the previous six months at least. My body depended on them, and I didn't know how to cope with life or how to fit back into my life back home. My body was ravaged. I weighed close to 100 pounds (my average is 130). I remember being so dead-tired that I could barely make it up the stairs; so tired in fact, that I'd actually have to crawl up them.

But I slowly made my way back to resembling someone that kind of seemed like me. I'd say the previous year and the year after were probably the hardest of my life. I had always been so determined to make something of myself, but then I went and did something like that. It was hard for me to wrap my head around and even harder for my family to understand.

The guilt I had from making my family worry so much was very hard to deal with. I continued to numb myself and escape with a legal drug; alcohol. It wasn't until my daughter was about two that I really started to make it less a part of my life. It was because of her that I realized I wanted to succeed and live up to my full potential. Not only for myself but to show her that she can do the same. I wanted to be as good of a role model as my mom.

I might not be the mother of the year, and I might not be the kind of parent my mom is, but I do believe we choose our parents for a reason. I know she chose me to help her grow into the powerful being she is meant to be. I take this responsibility very seriously.

CHAPTER 4

No matter what you do, you're divine

As I mentioned in the previous chapter, when I found yoga, it was like I had found something that had been missing my whole life. I realized that when I did yoga, I felt connected to something within that just...*knew*. It felt like an ancient part of myself yet very familiar.

I was coming home.

I was coming home to myself. Calling pieces of myself back that had been lost because of guilt, shame, regret, feelings of loss, betrayal, and from being made to feel less than enough. This was an amazing feeling but it started coming to me slowly. I definitely resisted it at first because it was such a new feeling. I doubted myself.

Am I really feeling these things?

Am I really connecting to something that's connected to Source?

A part of me that's had countless lifetimes?

A part of me that *knows* the answers and doesn't need to tirelessly look outside of myself to others for answers?

This can be scary! It can bring up a slew of questions that make you feel like you're doing something wrong, against beliefs that others around you hold, and you start to question yourself and doubt what you feel.

For some, they quit at this point. When stuff starts to bubble to the surface (because, in yoga, it always does) they get scared and quit instead of trusting the process and looking at what it is that is trying to be released.

I started with yoga at a gym. I've heard many people say that kind of yoga isn't "real" yoga--same with other types of power or hot yoga but I know it all has a place. We think we may know what is best for everyone, but so often we forget that all those beliefs are based on our personal experiences and our personal soul-makeup. We also have to remember that even though we think we know the answers and how the world works, there's NO way we can prove it. It's much easier to accept everyone and let them have their own beliefs about the world without judgment.

You work on you and the world around you will change. If you try to make others change and fit into your mold, you'll get very tired, very quickly.

The change starts within.

As you start to shine your light, others will be inspired to light theirs as well. And it might look nothing like your light. In fact, it's best that it doesn't! We don't need a billion clones running around; we need a billion people running around being **their** highest self. Doesn't that sound like an amazing world to live in?

So, no matter what type of yoga or spiritual practice you are doing, if it is helping you grow and is challenging you in new ways—mentally, physically, emotionally and spiritually—keep doing that until it doesn't challenge you anymore. When you feel like you've plateaued, seek out other forms of yoga or spiritual practice to reignite your passion for growth.

For me, yoga took a while to really start to change me on the outside. I have no doubt though, that it was working deep within, changing me on a spiritual, emotional, and mental level that I couldn't even comprehend. Every time you do a physical practice and move your body in new ways, you have the capacity to release residue that has been holding you back for years and years. It's like a wringing-out of the self. It's clearing out the cobwebs. It's shining light on all the dark spaces, breaking it completely apart, and allowing more light to enter.

It's *magic*. It's yoga.

After I moved back from California and got off the hard drugs, I still binge-drank and smoked cigarettes for ten more years until I finally got off them all (aside from a couple slides here and there) when my daughter was two. I knew that she was here to make a huge impact on the world, and I also knew that she deserved better than a mom who would choose to stay out drinking all night over her.

She absolutely, 100%, changed my life. She finally made me think about someone other than just me. Of course, I loved my family and my husband, but it's not the same. Not the same as having a perfect little soul counting on you to help make their life the best it can be. I took that very seriously.

Thank God I had my yoga and meditation to get me through that time of letting that part of me go. That part of me was so ingrained in my identity and who I was, and I knew I had to integrate positive habits and practices to completely rewire my brain.

But who are you if you're not the fun one? The crazy one? The one up for anything?

You have to reinvent yourself. But you have to do it in a way that is actually who you are meant to be; otherwise, you'll just have to eventually let that go, too and repeat the process all over again.

Yoga, meditation, and spiritual practices help you to drop the masks. They help you dig down to what is under it to find out who your soul really is, not who your ego says it is. This is the part of you that will always remain. It's there when you decide you're not the party girl anymore, it's there when you get wrinkles, it's there when you aren't "so-and-so's wife" or no longer a yoga teacher.

It's everlasting.

This is the part of you that I want to help you find. I want to save you some heartache or, at the very least, save you from going around in circles feeling lost and unsupported like I felt for years. In the following chapters, I will give you stories, tips, practices, and ideas to inspire and reignite your journey to *you*.

You *don't* have to do this alone.

This is a new era and women are stepping up to support each other, to drop the competition, drop the judgment, drop the comparisons. I'm assuming this is the type of woman you are or that you are working on trying to be; otherwise, you wouldn't have picked up this book. You're a woman who is *real*, who knows deep down that you don't need to be a size 2 to be a yogi, you don't need a $100 yoga mat or the perfect tight pants to do yoga, or that you can be 50 and just starting your spiritual journey.

No matter what "type" of woman you are, you are a Goddess. Just like me and just like my tribe. We come from every background, with regrets too many to count and a shit-ton of baggage. We come in different colors, shapes, and sizes, and yet we all have the same mission: to find our purpose and to . . .

Have the courage to live it.

You're able to read this book because of the amazing women who have already rallied around me and proved to me that there are so many of you out there that need to hear this call. I am so incredibly blessed to be supported by them so that I can support you.

Over the years, I've been incorporating many practices and beliefs into my spiritual routine to find things that really felt natural to me, so I could make it my own.

Too often, we're told that yoga, meditation, or other forms of spirituality have to look a certain way, and it's just not the case. It's time to tap back into your Intuition, that part of you that just KNOWS. I'll warn you, it's going to take some courage and a LOT of faith. So if you're ready for that, let's dive in!

If you haven't yet, make sure to come meet some of these amazing ladies in our free group. Gain access at www.yogagoddessacademy.com, introduce yourself and let us know you're reading this book.

Overcoming Fear

Fear is heavily rooted in the Muladhara or base chakra. Sure, it can make its home elsewhere, but I feel this is where it really lays down its roots. Fear is something I've struggled with for most of my life. I am definitely working through fears that have been deeply seeded in my being.

When I was only a little over the age of one, my father died suddenly and unexpectedly. I'm still not even sure of the extent of the wounds, but I am fairly certain this experience has contributed to my addictions and also how I tend to put a wall up around me. I tend to think that I can do everything on my own because that's what I learned through that experience.

I relied on my mother heavily for most of my life (and still do) but feel so much more secure in myself and find support from my connection to the Source instead of being able to find it only from her. That acceptance and love from my father that I had lost so early in life is re-emerging in a totally new way that isn't dependent on anyone yet allows me the capacity to fully love without expectations.

Since I've been surrounded by death since I was young, with my father dying and also because my caring mother would often visit the elderly in nursing homes with me by her side, I had to endure a lot of loss.

I developed a fear of death that has had a stronghold on me for quite some time. This fear shows up through hypochondria and low-grade OCD. It usually presents itself when I am overly stressed and over-committed so it's imperative to stay grounded and let go of what is causing me the most stress and anxiety.

Sometimes, it takes a while to figure out what those things are because our brains are amazing at hiding things from us that we don't want to look at!

I think even more than the fear of dying, it's the fear of my daughter growing up without a mother, like how I grew up without my dad. While I do have an amazing stepfather, the damage had already been done.

I am working daily to slow down my life and enjoy every minute. I am taking steps to working WAY less and doing things that aren't stressful, that I enjoy, WAY more.

Don't get me wrong, I could work on my business all day. I love it, and I love helping people, but I was finding that the more I focused on making money, the more stressed out by the whole thing I got.

So instead, I am working more on our family farm which not only helps me financially but brings me closer to my husband. By doing this, I can focus on creating content that will support my tribe instead of focusing on how to bring more money in. If you have a business, I highly recommend trying to switch to this frame of mind. It's totally different energetically and people can feel it!

I recommend finding things you enjoy doing that are low-stress. Stress is the one thing that will take us from healthy to extremely unhealthy. Most of us are in a constant state of fight or flight these days, with our never-ending to-do lists. We need to give our bodies time to heal through peaceful activities.

We must find time to enjoy life.

I've overcome so much and have had to do a lot of deep work to begin to feel like I'm making headway in healing and feeling whole. I wouldn't be where I am today if it weren't for my strong spiritual beliefs and practices.

Some beliefs that help me have less fear around death and sickness:

- I'll be going back to wherever I was before I was born.
- I am a spiritual being having a human experience.
- I'll see all my loved ones who have gone before me and will be greeted by them.
- Whatever I believe, that's what will manifest.
- I have much more control over my well-being than I think, I just have to remember.
- The body is an amazing machine and can heal anything as long as we have faith.

JOURNALING EXERCISE:

- What can you do every day to relax?
- How can you enjoy life more?
- What are some things you can cut out of your life that cause you stress?
- What are some hobbies you'd like to start?
- If you focus more on relaxing instead of the things that cause stress, how would your life look different?

- If you don't spend all your time focusing on your job, cleaning, looking a certain way, being the perfect mom, etc., what's the worst thing that could happen? The best thing?

CHAPTER 5

What's really important?

During the most recent retreat I led in Costa Rica, with an amazing group of women, I realized a few things about how I want to live my life. On a retreat, especially if you're the one leading it, you don't know what you're going to get out of it because that's not really the goal. The goal is to support the women and build a nurturing, comfortable environment where they can get vulnerable and grow.

I am so lucky to have such amazing women in my tribe. Even though, yes, I created that space, they held ME in that space with them. It was amazing. I got way more out of the retreat than I could have expected.

One thing I realized was how far I've come in the past couple of years. I've led other retreats and done other things in my business and while they were satisfactory, they weren't as great as I knew they could be. This retreat definitely showed me, without a doubt, how far I've grown, but not only that, also what I am attracting into my experience and how that's changed and evolved as well.

A couple of the things I realized on the retreat:

- I want to spend more time in nature.
- I need to be more present.
- I make WAY too big of a deal out of things that don't really matter in the long run.
- I need to focus on the things that DO matter in the long run, like my family, friends, and passions.
- I need to unplug *way* more often.
- I am really good at making people laugh (often at my expense, but hey, it's always worth it to make people laugh until they almost pee their pants).
- I need to show the world more of the REAL me.

Let's dig into each of these a bit more.

I want to spend more time in nature. It's SUPER easy for me to become ungrounded. I am airy and watery and love new, shiny things that easily distract me from what I am trying to focus on. Being in nature helps me to connect to my center and get aligned with my soul, so I can more easily remember what's important to me in my life and to not stress too much over the little things. While I go for walks almost every day in the summer, I have decided to also work on our family farm more which will help my husband and me be closer while also getting me out in the dirt a few days a week. I've also been helping my daughter create a fairy garden outside which has been super fun, and it lets her imagination run wild. Which leads me to my next point.

Be more present. This means, to me personally, to SLOW DOWN--to enjoy the little moments. My mother has really shown me how to do this. She never rushes my daughter when she's working on things and using her imagination. So now, instead of looking at the time and rushing those precious moments together (the ones that will stay with both of us for the rest of our lives), I sit and breathe in the air, I notice the surrounding nature, I smile and feel gratitude for another day that I get to be her mother.

I make WAY too big of a deal out of things that don't really matter in the long run. Does it REALLY matter if I get one more blog post up today? What about if I make a four-course dinner from scratch? Maybe I should stress about not posting on Instagram for five days now? What did that one girl's comment MEAN on my post? Why isn't such and such calling me back? Did I piss her off?

Ugh! Enough.

THIS. SHIT. DOESN'T. MATTER. Seriously, it doesn't. Our ego thinks it does, but you must get control over your thoughts. It is a practice. Just like yoga. It takes time but is SO worth it. The benefits you'll receive from just letting the petty shit go will seriously change your life.

JOURNALING EXERCISE:

- What are you ready to stop stressing over?
- What pettiness drives you nuts about other people?
- How are those things just mirrors reflecting back to you what you don't want to see in yourself anymore? *(Not fun, I know, but a GREAT practice.)*

I need to focus on the things that DO matter in the long run like my family, friends, and passions. It's easy to SAY these words but still be super caught up in the drama of life. Let's do ourselves both a favor and make this lifetime really count. Most of us aren't dealing with many factors that humans have had to deal with in the past. We don't have to worry about famine, bears chasing us, or freezing to death. But it seems like our minds will always find *something* to stress about which takes away from the simple pleasures of life. Every time your mind goes to the drama, bring it back to what you are grateful for in your life. This act alone will cause miracles. It may take a while to find your passions again but trust me, they're there and guess what? You don't even need to be "good" at them! The only prerequisite is that you feel joy.

I need to unplug WAY more often. This one is huge, and I hear it from so many women in my tribe as well. It's so easy to get caught up in the drama of social media. While it helps me to make amazing connections to incredible women, feeling tethered and available at ALL times really zaps my energy and gets me out of alignment very quickly.

Remember the days when we didn't even have cell phones? If

someone wanted to get a hold of us, they'd leave a message for us on our machines at home. Then, when we were ready, we'd call them back. We didn't have a little notification on Facebook telling us that we need to reply to messages faster to be a good business person. I say "F" that. I'm taking a stand and hope you will, too. I took messenger off my phone as well as notifications for email and Facebook. People can wait.

Your peace of mind is way more important and will help you be a better person or business person in the long run because it will keep you shining more brightly. If these tips don't work, try installing an app that actually keeps you off your phone for a set amount of time. Only allowing yourself to hop on a few times per day and for an allotted time frame, maybe 10-15 minutes, after which, you'll get back to your day.

This may take some getting used to because we've been conditioned to have #FOMO (fear of missing out) but it's oh so worth it. We need to be examples for the younger generations.

I am really good at making people laugh (often at my expense, but hey, it's *always* worth it to make people laugh until they almost pee their pants). Well, I'm sitting here deciding how much I really want to share with the world through this book, but I'm figuring that if I'm going to write a book, it might as well show the REAL--like, really real--me.

I thought that over the years I was really showing the real me. Then when we were on our trip, I realized that there were parts of me that I wasn't letting others see. Since I'm a yoga and spiritual teacher, I wanted people to take me seriously. I didn't even realize I was doing this!

When we were on this last retreat, I told a couple of stories that

I've only told maybe one other person, my soul sister, Suzanne. She urged me to tell them about this experience I had to see if anyone else thought the same. Now, just because they laughed their asses off, I'm definitely not having high hopes that you will, too.

This may very well be the point in the book where you put it down, never to pick it up again. Then again, if you've been there, then you'll be my soul sister for life and that's a chance I'm willing to take. Why? Because it's WAY more valuable to have a FEW people who know and love the real you than a million people who love a fake version of you.

The story as I told it for the first time to Suzanne was posed as a question that I asked her out of pure curiosity to see if she experienced the same feeling as me in this particular situation. It's something that most people would never have spoken about out loud, probably because they have way better manners that I do but anyway . . .

Here goes.

You know it's going to be a good day when you're in the shower in the morning and, while washing your, ahem, butt crack, you find a nice, long hair that must have slid down your back while washing your hair and into the crevice of your ass. There's just not a better feeling in the world, one that is more satisfying, than pulling that hair out from where it doesn't belong.

OK, OK, I know! Gross right? But c'mon. If you've *ever* had long hair don't try to act like you don't know what I'm talking about. Don't be bitchy like that.

Moving on . . .

I need to show the world more of the REAL me. Uh, see above. You think I WANT to put shit like that in a book for everyone to see? Not really. But I follow my Intuition (which you'll learn how to do more and more as you read this book) and I know from experience that when I share more of the REAL me, the more I find my true soul sisters and the more I can help them be brave enough to start sharing their light.

Also, by sharing more of the real me, you will see that if I can be a Goddess, well, then any woman can! Trust me, my husband has told me that I "burp like a trucker" more than once. I cuss like a sailor, too.

But only around those I love. And I pretty much love everyone so . . . Watch out world!

Other reasons why it's important to share the *real* you:

- It's therapeutic for YOU!
- It helps other women know that you don't have to be PERFECT to be a "Goddess."
- It paves the way for other women to shine their unique light.
- It gives other women confidence that if you can do it, so can they!
- It's much easier to live a life that's authentic than trying to live up to an image of perfection that is unattainable.
- It will make you more and more confident, happy, and content with your life.

CHAPTER 6

Healing the Self

As I write this book, huge shifts are happening for me and old traumas are coming up because of it. I'm having physical symptoms that cause me great anxiety because, well, I'm a hypochondriac--I'll admit it. I've been conditioned to feel like anxiety is normal and that it's my "normal." But I don't want it to be my "normal" anymore.

I'm doing a lot of work to bring up old energies that are stuck in my body. They're hiding in the shadows and whether I'm ready or not, they're being kicked out of their hiding places.

As we cleanse our energetic bodies, our auras, these old experiences and traumas will undoubtedly work their way up to the surface. Now, this can oftentimes be something that happens seemingly out of nowhere. We may not have consciously been trying to release a certain trauma but as we continue with our spiritual path, it is just a natural byproduct of the process.

This could also be similar to the experience of "kundalini rising." Kundalini is an energy that rests at the base of the spine. When you start making shifts and growing, this energy starts to rise. It can cause a lot of disturbances in your life because it will clear away whatever is in the way. When this happens, a lot of people get a bit freaked out because they don't know how to put it into words or have anyone to talk to about it.

Either way, I urge you to stick with your practices when things start to get icky and trust me, they will. That just means you are awakening, cleansing, purifying, and now more than ever, you need to dedicate more time to your spiritual practices than ever before to deal with any symptoms that may arise.

Just to give you an idea of the symptoms that could come up, I'll share some that I've experienced:

- Extreme anxiety
- Obsessive thoughts
- Fear
- Helplessness
- Hopelessness
- Feelings of dishonor and abandonment by loved ones
- Grief

All of these are resulting in physical symptoms such as:

- Heart palpitations
- Fluttering in the heart chakra
- Chest pains
- Fatigue

How do I know these symptoms are because of what's going on emotionally and energetically? Because I continue to get signs and be led to experiences that are helping me uncover and learn why all of this is happening. But even more than that, I am listening to my Inner Guide. When I really sit and listen, I don't feel scared, I don't feel that it's stemming from something physical, and the more I learn, the more I realize that most, if not all, physical issues stem from emotional or energetic issues.

I was led to pick up a book that I've had on my shelf for quite some time called *You Can Heal Your Life,* by Louise Hay. She explains that so much of our physical issues come from holding onto resentment, blame, etc.--that if we would only forgive, we would be able to heal SO much.

She says that we need to start with those that we find the HARDEST to forgive because that's really what's causing us the most pain and is holding us back from having the life and the health we truly desire.

I'm also learning from one of my newer teachers, Sonia Choquette, that we hold these memories, these traumas, not in our cells as previously thought, but in the morphogenic field around the cells. This field also surrounds our entire physical body and is more often called our *aura*.

The aura is starting to get more recognition as something that is real and can have an impact on us, especially when we start to learn how to cleanse and release these old experiences and beliefs FROM it. As I stated above, as we begin doing our inner work, these old things that are hanging onto our energetic field are nudged into releasing. Sonia explains that as they are nudged, they may begin to bubble up to the surface, and then we may experience a lot of those same emotions that are attached to that situation.

This might be confusing to us as we're not really sure where these old emotions are coming from or why we are having anxiety or other symptoms. What I am finding is that it's super important to have faith in the process, to have faith in something greater than yourself. We chose to come into this physical experience and, if you're reading this book, you've chosen to do spiritual work so that you can do what you feel you came here to do.

We must have faith that this is all part of that learning and that we are actually asking for it. I always tell my yoga students, especially the yoga teacher trainees, that this path isn't always rainbows and sunshine. Chances are, there will be some major muck that you are going to have to deal with but it's all for an important reason. You wouldn't be able to shine as brightly as you do now or as you WANT to if you didn't start to clear out the cobwebs if you didn't deal with the shadows.

This reminds me of why I love practicing and teaching the lotus mudra. The baby lotus gets barely any light down at the bottom of a pond but it has faith that if it starts popping up through the muck and mud and through the murky waters, that it will find sunlight at the top where it can bloom into its full beauty.

The same is true for this work you chose to do. It won't always be fun or easy, but think about how great it will feel when you can blossom and share your true authentic beauty and gifts with the world, unencumbered by your past traumas, experiences, and old beliefs about yourself and what you are capable of in this life.

Practices to Heal

Practice lotus mudra by bringing the hands together in a prayer position. Keep the outer parts of the palm, thumbs, and pinky fingers together as you open the middle of the palms and extend the middle three fingers of each hand up and out like a blooming flower.

Move your body in new ways to release old energy. Dance, yoga, Qi Gong, Tai Chi. Any sort of movement will do but the easiest thing to do is to dance like absolutely NO one is watching, moving in the weirdest ways you can think of and in ways your body has never moved before! This will get into those murky areas and start the process of release.

Make some noise! Crank up your favorite jam and sing your heart out! Alternatively, you could do some OMs, some loud sighs, or even yell like a banshee! Again, the crazier you get, the better it's going to feel!

Breathe. Take long, deep inhales and long, deep exhales. See how many counts your inhale takes then let your exhale be one to three counts longer than your inhale.

Sit or lay with your eyes closed, in a quiet room, and visualize healing light coming into your body through the crown of the head. As you inhale, let this light permeate your cells, releasing and cleansing anything that is stuck. Exhale and visualize gray air moving out of your mouth and releasing from your body.

When Did You Lose the Connection?

Within my online community, I uncover a lot of interesting similarities among the tribe members. A while back we were reading "Code Red" by Lisa Lister. This book brought up a lot of stuff for many of us. I highly recommend it for this reason. In this society, and as women, we have to hide so much about just BEING women. It's not considered polite to talk about your period because it may make others, usually men, uncomfortable.

When did this come about? Did we stop talking about it because it was actually a source of our power as women?

Around the time of periods, we have heightened psychic and empathic abilities as well as a deeper connection to our emotions. While to others we may seem wild around the time of our periods, if we honor ourselves instead of pushing through, acting like we don't need more rest or to let out a good cry, we inhibit the natural connection that we do have to our inner Goddess, our Intuition.

Many in my tribe found a striking, and albeit, depressing, similarity. We found that when we were the age around puberty that we were taught to dim our lights. When we looked back, we realized that around that time, we had an inner knowing that started to surface.

I remember having a new fascination with Wicca and even purchased a book on the subject. Looking back, I know it was a call, a remembering, from my Spirit. I know now from years of being on this path that I have a deep connection to the Earth and how we can harness her energy to manifest and shape our reality.

Others in the group remembered similar but different things that they were drawn to, maybe astrology, oracle cards, spirit guides, etc. And the sad thing? We were all shot down in one way or another, all made to feel silly, weird, or even "bad" for even bringing the ideas up.

At that precious age, most do not want to be different. We want to fit. Fear of being an outcast is pretty much the guiding force at that time in most young women's lives, so we learn to stop trusting our instincts.

But where does it come from? Is it something ancient in our spirit's past? An energy current running through the history of the world? Maybe in our bloodline and DNA? Who knows? But it's there and it's undeniable. We're scared to rise.

As women, we've been burned at the stake for speaking our truth. We've been banished, tortured, forsaken by our families. We've learned that if it's *not* a safe thing to do, often times, we don't.

Goddess, I want to tell you that now more than ever, is THE safest time for you to rise up and speak your truth. Most of us are fortunate enough to live in a country where we won't be killed for speaking our truth. If you are one of the lucky ones, it's your duty (and probably the reason you chose to be born where you were) to uncover and strengthen your unique voice.

A good place to start is to listen to your Intuition so you can develop a healthy relationship with it. Then comes the work on the throat chakra. There is more about the throat chakra in coming pages but simply put, you can strengthen this chakra by beginning to use your voice more than staying quiet but also balance it out by truly and deeply listening to others. Speaking your voice should be done with love. It's not just saying whatever is on your mind. It comes from a place of love, not ego, so you must listen to your inner self before anything.

Within my group, I encourage women to start rising. It is a safe place to do so, and many women practice there before going out and sharing with the world. I highly recommend you find a tribe of sisters who will support you, encourage you, and lift you up.

Uncovering Intuition

The first time in my adult life that I really remember feeling and leaning into my Intuition was when I adopted a plant-based diet in my early 20s. That really led me down a totally new path that had me feeling like my eyes were really opening, and I was becoming aware of a whole host of things that I felt were being kept from the public. Things like how animals that are raised for food are treated and how our environment is getting polluted. These things are unpleasant and back then, they weren't talked about nearly as much as they are today. I am SO grateful for this shift!

I feel like going plant-based was really the mark of my deep spiritual journey and period of extreme personal growth. The shifts in perception alone kick-started something within me that connected me more and more to who I really was.

I then followed my inner voice and began yoga. Soon after that, I embarked on my year-long yoga teacher training. I had struggled for most of my young adult life not knowing what in the hell I was going to do with my life. At that point, I was still lost, still living the rock-and-roll lifestyle, but at least I was beginning my journey of awakening.

After I became a yoga instructor, I started teaching a few classes per week, building my confidence as a teacher. During this time, my husband became increasingly interested in quitting his software engineering job and moving back home to where we both grew up to do organic farming.

This was quite a scary and risky life change and a lot of people told us we were crazy to leave the comforts of his job behind, but we knew that there was more to life than trying to "keep up with the Jones'" and that's always how we felt up in the suburbs, like all that mattered was making more money and getting nicer things.

We didn't fit into that way of thinking and it was sucking the life out of us.

So we listened to our Intuition and moved three hours south to begin a year-long internship program at a highly-reputable and well-run organic vegetable farm near Champaign-Urbana. I worked on the farm and taught yoga at local gyms and yoga studios which gave me more practice with working with different types of students in different settings, which was great.

The next step was to begin our own farm. We finally did it! I'd say starting this farm and struggling to make it work was the hardest thing we've done as a couple. It's definitely a testament to our love for each other that we stayed together through all of it!

We soon after had our daughter. I remember my water breaking as I was doing the dishes in this old, rickety farmhouse that was 45 minutes from the hospital. The drive to said hospital was probably the worst ride of my life! Every little bump sent bolts of pain through my body!

I was guided to have a natural birth without any drugs and thank God, we found an awesome doula who could support both my husband and myself during the process. My husband was great and helped the whole time--except for when he looked like he was going to faint, the doula made him take a break!

After we brought her home, I focused on getting my body back to normal while taking care of her as best I could. I am lucky that I had so much support from both sets of our parents. We are truly blessed.

After about three years in that old, cold, drafty house, we bought my husband's parents' house--the one he grew up in--and thankfully, moved there. Raising my daughter in that old house was definitely not something I was excited about. I remember going down to the bathroom in the middle of the night and being able to see my breath and I had to keep my daughter wrapped up like a burrito in her infant car seat to keep her warm! We were poor, to say the least. But it's what we asked for. We didn't want to just live the life that everyone had set out for us or what we thought we "should" do, we wanted to do something meaningful.

This was all a part of the learning process, and we had to struggle in order to, one day, be able to appreciate how far we'd come.

During this time I was content being a housewife and a mom. I was also teaching a couple yoga classes here and there at the local park district but I didn't have any grandiose ideas about what I could really do in my life with my talents. I was planning on just helping with the farm and getting my hand more in with the marketing aspects. I did this for a while but then realized that I wasn't feeling fulfilled.

As a newer yoga teacher, I didn't know any other steps or ways to progress in my profession besides opening a yoga studio. I thought that was the only next step. Then someone mentioned to me that I should open one and I knew there weren't any studios in my area yet at the time, so that's what I did!

Even though it turned out to be something that I didn't want to do forever, I can't tell you what all that experience taught me, it's just so much.

Some things I learned that I want you to realize, too:

1. Never compare yourself to what others are doing, you do *you* and it will work out.
2. Don't watch what others are doing because it will just make you veer off your authentic path.
3. Don't worry about what others are saying about you or if they're copying you. If this is happening, you must be doing something right.
4. As you shine your light brighter and put yourself more

in the spotlight, some people are going to be intimidated by that and have anger toward you. That's THEIR issue, not yours.

5. Have confidence in yourself.
6. You ARE good enough, just trust me.
7. You ARE capable.
8. You CAN run a successful business.
9. You CAN be an inspiring leader.
10. You ARE a great teacher.

Now, your path may not be to open a business, the point is that YOU can do anything you set your mind to. I know you've heard that a billion times in a billion ways, but you guys, it's fucking true. Now if only you believed in yourself enough to LET yourself have that faith. Just THINK of what your life could look like!

Instead of eating shit sandwiches for breakfast, you could be shitting rainbows. It's all a matter of perspective, and ya know what?

It's ALL up to you.

Every. Single. Thing.

Every. Single. Thought.

Doing the Work

I know, it can be hard to swallow. Thinking that everything in your life, every decision, every experience, every feeling you FEEL is All. Up. To. YOU.

It's so much easier to take the route of blame, resentment, and fear--saying all these excuses that are holding you back from being the person you set forth to come here to *be*.

Why are you keeping yourself small? Chances are, the main reason is a lack of confidence. Somewhere you learned that you aren't good enough, smart enough, capable enough, resourceful enough or that you don't even deserve to have these things because you've fucked up in your past.

Well, ya know what? THAT'S ALL BULLSHIT!

All those lies you believe about yourself. Bullshit. You have the power to change every one of those limiting beliefs but it's not just going to magically happen one day. You'll never wake up and say, "Oh my gosh, ya know what? I'm totally fucking confident now, and I am ready to get out there and kick some major ass! Oh, and also, I, all of a sudden, don't give a FUCK what anyone thinks about me anymore! Holy shit, it's a miracle!"

Guess what. There's no magic pill.

There's no easy way to do it. It takes work and it's called spiritual and personal development.

It's called digging deep, clearing out the shadows and the cobwebs, and staring those fuckers straight in their googly-eyes. Don't get me wrong. I'm not mad at the shadows for being there. They have a purpose. They help our egos make sense out of life and keep us safe at that moment.

We don't want to be safe anymore. We don't want to "play" safe anymore. We want to live BIG. And whether those shadows don't want to have your light shine on them or not . . . Momma, Goddess, it's time.

Making the Work a Priority

We are living in an age where we are constantly in the fight or flight mode. Without enough time for us to fully relax, we are setting ourselves up for sickness. Burning the candle at both ends isn't glamorous, and we need to stop making it seem as though it is.

There is so much pressure put on us by those around us (and mostly by ourselves) to do better, do more, add one more thing to our plate, but it's killing us. The symptoms will show up emotionally first, which is a sign of where we *are* with our emotions, but they will eventually manifest in the body if we don't do anything about it.

This is a new age, and WE are the ones who need to help make the shift on the planet and that shift will have deep roots in self-care. There are more yoga teachers, energy healers, and lightworkers than ever before, but don't let that discourage you. We're NEEDED more than ever before to help show the way--to break the molds of all this fast-paced living and give tools for relaxation, rest, and regeneration.

I believe we are about to enter a dramatic time of healing on this planet. Every day, more people's lights are starting to turn on and it's our duty to face our fears, get over ourselves, and be a beacon for others just waiting for someone like you to give them permission to turn on theirs.

Now, we know no one needs permission, but by others seeing YOU stepping into your fear, seeing YOU walk the path, seeing YOU being the RAF Goddess that you are, you will inspire more people than you could even imagine. You might never know how many people you inspire because not everyone is at a point yet where they feel comfortable telling you. You have to trust that this is why you're here. You know this. In some ways, you've *always* known.

How can you start finding more time to nourish and nurture your God Pod? (This is a loving term I got from Kris Carr in one of her books years ago.)

When you can devote more of your time to self-care daily, you will not only inspire and give others permission to do the same, but you will connect to something much deeper than your mind and ego (which usually control our every move). You'll connect and tap in to your Authentic Self, Source, your Inner Guru, your Intuition. The you that chose to come into this body in the first place, with these parents and situations, to help you grow.

The YOU that will *always* be even after the physical body has returned to the earth.

Some activities I am adding into my days to find more joy and to de-stress are:

- Writing
- Unplugging more often
- Meditating longer
- Reading spiritual books
- Chanting with or without my harmonium
- Learning how to play the guitar
- Spending more time in nature

- Cooking healthy meals with as much food from our farm as possible
- Doing releasing or visualizations daily
- More consistent yoga
- Taking Epsom salt and essential oil baths

Some things I'm doing less to help me stay balanced:

- Watching less T.V.
- Never watching the news
- Really being aware of the energy I am letting near me
- Letting go of relationships that are not filling my cup
- Crossing things off my list that don't really need to be done
- Spending time on only the things that will move my business forward instead of on a lot of things that just fill my time
- Feeling like I always need to be "doing" something

This may all take up a lot of time, but when you take a good hard look at your life, like I did, and usually in mid-life, you start to realize what's important.

When you see how many people around you are sick or super stressed or pissed off at the world, you realize you don't want to be like that. You remember somewhere deep down, how life can really be lived. You just have to be one of the brave ones that don't let society's idea of how a woman should live her life have an effect on you. You have been chosen to lead the way.

Are you ready?

Think about it, in the grand scheme of things does it really matter if you are a size 8? Does it really matter if you spend all day working on your business when you could get the most important things done in two hours and spend the rest of the day doing things you enjoy? Why do we feel so much guilt around doing things that make us happy? Why are we proud to say how busy we are?

Let's shift this way of thinking. We must all do it together. Next time someone asks you how you are, try not to talk about how busy you are or complain. Instead, say how you are trying to find more time to relax and what you are doing to make this happen. This might get you some weird looks but it will have a ripple effect. Even if it doesn't sink in with those you tell it to right away, they might think about it later in their day and have second thoughts about how they are living their life.

Let's start a movement where we don't let our lives pass us by and let's support each other in this! Give women props when they do good things for themselves, don't judge, don't be jealous.

Looking at the Shadow-Self

One of the biggest ways we can start to grow is by looking at our shadows. It's easy to do the surface-spiritual work, which is what I feel I've been doing for most of the past 15 years of my journey, but that's necessary work. You can't start on your path and dive right into your issues with abandonment, that you developed at a young age when your dad died, that you then unknowingly placed onto the relationship with your brother, for example. Because you're not READY for that work yet.

On our spiritual journey and throughout our lives, we'll uncover layers and layers and layers of this stuff. Work we thought we were totally done and over with, then *bam*, God shows us we have even more to learn on that subject.

For me, one of the surface ideas I thought I had down pat was loving everyone. I am very good at this. I can love almost anyone despite what kind of person they are because I know we are all just humans going through this spiritual experience and that we all are basically doing the best we can with what we have. We may not think others are doing the best they can from our outside perspective, but they are just trying to make it through life in a way that makes sense to their brains and their emotions because of what they've been through in their life.

I get this.

Then I realized there's a whole other layer to it. And the funny thing is, I keep asking for growth so why in the hell do I keep getting surprised when I get blindsided by situations that test me? It's when I remember that this is what I asked for that I can get out of my own way and learn from the experience.

You have to step aside, you have to put your ego in the back seat and get out of the "why me" mentality because, let me tell you, sister, that's not going to get you ANYwhere that you want to go. It may seem like it's protecting you in the short term but it's keeping you small and it's keeping your light dim. It's doing more harm than good but the ego will always tell you differently because that's its

JOB: to keep you safe.

When you recognize this is happening, politely tell your ego to take a back seat, that you'll take the wheel on this one from here. Then comes the fun part... You get to look at why these things affect you so much. Why do you often react so negatively to that person or situation? Is it bringing something up within yourself that maybe you don't like because you know you have a little of the same behavior within you? You think, "Of course not! I would never be like that!" But then look past those thoughts. That's still your ego trying to make you look good to yourself. It seems like it's a nice thing for it to do but really it's just keeping you small.

The biggest thing we can do here is to:

NOT REACT. Do not explode.

Gather yourself up and back away from the situation.

Cool down by doing something that will get you back into alignment like singing, dancing like a crazy person, yelling at the top of your lungs (alone, in your house, of course), yoga, or running. Anything to help you blow off steam will do.

After you've gotten into alignment, meditate for at least 20 minutes at a time to really get the effects. I find it takes about 10 minutes for the mind to even settle down. If you want to figure this shit out, just do it, mkay?

Journal about why it bothered you so much. Look at it from the angle of how it made you feel, not "They did this, they did that, that's why they suck."

Once you get "those" feelings down, dive deeper, and look at where else you have felt that way in your life. Who made you feel that way when you were younger? What situations made you feel those things were true about you?

If you've made it this far, girl, you are doing great and will grow in ways you didn't think possible. Things will start to just roll off your shoulder instead of getting you fired up, hurt, or making you shut down! Wouldn't that be great?

Now that you've realized why these things upset you so much, you can see them more for what they really are and forgive the situation a lot easier. The situations or people that are upsetting you so much now are NOT the ones that made you feel this way in your past, so stop putting all the years of blame into this scenario.

Journal about those past experiences, do yoga, have your own rituals, go to therapy, get energy healing, release that shit any way you can.

Send love to this current situation and/or person (as well as the past versions). Forgive. Repeat this often, as many times as needed until you feel a shift. You might be surprised to find they shift their energy toward you as well. This happens a lot and is a very nice side-effect of you doing the work.

Give yourself some much-needed props for stepping into a whole new you. One that is ready to stop being the victim and start taking life and all its experiences by the balls.

The fascinating ego can try to "help" in numerous ways. Keeping us locked in a state of fear is its best friend. We get it, Ego, you're trying to keep us safe!

If you don't pay attention, you can find your ego getting out of control in ways such as:

- Complaining
- Judging or criticizing others
- Acting like your shit don't stink
- Telling lies
- Making others feel small

You. The Powerful.

Everyone is powerful but
Only some of us choose to really believe it to be true.
You are more powerful than your wildest dreams.
Don't waste another day not seeing the power, the
beauty, that Source sees in you.

Stepping into Fear

The first thing to realize is that it's OK to feel fear. If you didn't
feel fear, you might be a sociopath so rest easier knowing that. I've
spent a lot of time over the years facing my fears and stepping into
them. It is *not* fun but the rewards are amazing.

I am always so proud of myself for putting myself out there, for
asking for opportunities, for taking those opportunities and sharing
more and more of the real me because it helps me grow. I've grown
more over the past five years than in my entire life, I'd say, because
I am doing it consciously. I am surrendering to my dharma, to my
Divine Purpose and when you do that, you have to realize that you'll

continue to get more experiences to help you grow into the person you came here to bc.

Success is the difference between feeling the fear and letting it stop you and feeling thc fcar and moving forward anyway. What are you letting hold you back from stepping into it? Is it a fear of:

- Judgment?
- Unworthiness?
- Failing?
- Looking like a dumbass?
- Shining too bright?
- Making others feel bad?

Look in there and pull these things out. Take away their power by shining your spiritual flashlight on them. Once you do this, you can see things in a clearer perspective and you'll have a better chance at seeing why it's so silly to hold onto those things that aren't serving you anymore.

If you're reading this book, you *know* you have something to share with the world and you know that never stepping into and through the fear isn't going to get you where you want to be so grab your journal and start writing down everything that is holding you back from stepping into your truest potential.

You may want to write about where those things came from. What past experiences made you feel that way about yourself? Then get into why you don't need to hold on to them anymore and finally, write about how your life will look different once you start doing the work to release these limiting beliefs.

CHAPTER 7

Grow Some Ovaries, Why Don't Ya?

Why in the hell do people say to "Grow some balls"? Who the fuck would want those weak ass things dangling, all exposed, just waiting to get the slightest touch which will make you drop to your knees in pain?

No, thanks. I'll keep my badass lady parts, thank you very much.

Don't discount what you've been given. You're tougher than you think. Now you just need to learn how to have confidence in yourself. You need to start the process of letting go of feelings of unworthiness, self-doubt, and self-loathing.

Look back over your life and all you've been through. Have you come out of the other side of many challenging situations? I'm sure you have. Why don't you give yourself the credit you deserve for how far you've come? Sure, you may still be in the middle of some challenges but, if you look back, you can see your undeniable growth. Take some time to appreciate what you've achieved.

JOURNALING PROMPT:

- What have you overcome already in your lifetime?
- What are you proud of yourself for?
- How have you grown over the past year?
- The past three years?
- The past 10 years?
- What would you tell your younger self?

Now that you're starting to believe in yourself a little more, let's take it a few steps further. Let me share with you some things I've learned along the way that have made me more confident and can help you do the same.

1. Confidence doesn't just happen. You HAVE to put yourself in situations that will make you practice being confident. So...
2. Fake confidence until you have it. There will always be situations that will push you past your comfort zones but, with practice, the things you once saw as something you could never

do will become old hat. Then you'll start getting bigger and scarier opportunities that you can draw from all your past experiences and be better equipped to step into them.

3. You'll never wake up one day and say, "Oh yes! I'm finally completely and utterly 100% confident and sure of myself! Yes!!" The only way this happens is if you follow numbers 1 and 2.

4. Stop comparing yourself to others. You might *think* that others have it all figured out or all their shit put together, but trust me, they don't. Over the years, I've spoken with countless women who, from the outside, appear to have it all together. Or they're talking about how they are looking at these other women who have it all together, but they DON'T. So just stop it. Everyone will be more "put together" in different ways. It's those things that just come easy or are fun to us that we are able to make look like it's a piece of cake, because, to us, it is. So why compare yourself to someone who is just naturally gifted at that one thing? If you looked hard enough, you'd see that SHE envies how you can so gracefully do some things you do. Which leads me to my next point.

5. Find what comes easy to you and focus on building that skill. If possible, find others that you can outsource those other tasks to. Doing every single thing that needs to be done won't make you Mom of the Year or Business Woman of the Year so cut yourself some slack.

6. Ask for help and get over your inability to receive love, help, or support. If this is something that is hard for you, DO THE WORK. If you continue trying to be superwoman, you'll end up

fizzling out and it could be something small like needing a week in bed, or it could end up something much larger and scarier, so do yourself a favor and deal with that shit now before it comes back and bites you in the ass.

Leaning In

One of my favorite ways to stay on track and aligned spiritually is to focus on "leaning in." If something doesn't make me feel good, I don't lean into it, I don't follow it down the path. If something DOES feel good, I DO lean into it.

Our feelings and emotions do not define us, they're not even us. But they ARE the biggest indicators that let us know if we are in alignment with Spirit or not. Instead of attaching yourself to your emotions, try to stand on the outside a bit and look at the emotions objectively.

Ask yourself some questions like:

- Why do I feel this way?
- How can I change my reaction to the situation next time?
- Can I avoid situations like this in the future? How?
- If I do attract a similar person or experience again, what tools have I now learned to better deal with the situation?

When you are at a lower vibrating emotion, the best thing you can do to is to try to get to a higher vibrating place. It's our initial thought to try to jump to the vibration or emotion the furthest away. If you're in total despair, you may want to jump all the way up to loving life and being in complete and utter joy, but that is an extremely challenging thing to do, and when you CAN'T get there right away, you may become discouraged and delve even deeper into despair and sadness.

Instead, try to bring yourself up just a tiny bit. Hang out there for a while, and when you're able to stay there for a bit, then work on coming up just a little more. I love this scale from the book *Ask and It is Given*. Use it the next time you are feeling down in the dumps and are having a hard time lifting up your vibe.

1. Joy/Appreciation/Empowered/Freedom/Love
2. Passion
3. Enthusiasm/Eagerness/Happiness
4. Positive Expectation/Belief
5. Optimism
6. Hopefulness
7. Contentment
8. Boredom
9. Pessimism
10. Frustration/Irritation/Impatience
11. Overwhelmed
12. Disappointment
13. Doubt
14. Worry
15. Blame

16. Discouragement

17. Anger

18. Revenge

19. Hatred/Rage

20. Jealousy

21. Insecurity/Guilt/Unworthiness

22. Fear/Grief/Depression/Despair/Powerlessness

If you find yourself in guilt or unworthiness, try to move yourself up to jealousy or even hatred or rage. I know that sounds a bit counterintuitive but I'm not asking you to STAY in those emotions, I just want you to get out of the place where you've been stuck.

Some activities that help me get my vibe up are:

- Dancing like no one is watching
- Singing like no one is listening
- Cleaning or organizing (I don't LOVE the ACT of doing these things usually, but I *do* love the feeling after!)
- Playing or making crafts with my daughter
- Doing yoga
- Meditating
- Listening to Abraham-Hicks audio recordings on YouTube
- Listening to spiritual audiobooks
- Watching spiritual, uplifting, or funny movies
- Calling an inspiring friend

- Helping others

High Vibe Living

I remember when I first wanted to try out this "High Vibe" way of life. I knew that eating a lot of fresh, raw foods is key to living like this so, a couple years after going vegan, I tried out a raw diet for a couple of months.

It was a fucking disaster.

Mind you, this was in the early 2000s when all this stuff wasn't spoken about nearly as much as it is now. The term "vegan" wasn't even well-known then, so I was really kind of going into this blindly. I wasn't as in love with vegetables as I am now and fruit would get kind of boring, so I relied heavily on nuts and seeds.

Do you know what happens when you eat that much fat? I'll tell you what happens. You shit your brains out, that's what.

I remember that something I was really fascinated with was using this diet to kill all sorts of nasty parasites that take up residence in your body. There were all sorts of pictures, online and in the books I was reading about the raw food diet, of dead parasites coming out in people's poo.

Needless to say, I was excited at the prospect.

This story doesn't have a happy ending, though. No parasites were ever seen as I did the whole thing completely wrong and gave up before I saw any real value.

The reason I'm telling you this story and many of the other fucked up shit I'm divulging is because I want you to know that these things don't always come easily. You're not going to wake up one day and have the most perfect, clean, vegan, organic, local, non-GMO diet that there ever was. It takes time and honestly, if you strive for perfection, it will probably blow up in your face and cause you so much stress that will totally negate all the good foods you're eating.

Before we get into the "Hows," let's get into what in the hell a high-vibe lifestyle is and why you'd want to live one anyway.

In order for our bodies to perform optimally, we have to supply it with foods that will support it. Duh. But there are so many people saying so many things that it's hard to decipher what you should be doing from what you shouldn't. I get it.

When I went through my training to become a certified health coach through the Institute of Integrative Nutrition, I used that time to A) begin a serious, daily meditation practice and B) learn how to be more healthy myself.

Something I didn't expect to come out of it was how I started to actually cut myself some slack around what I ate. I was always trying to have this perfect diet, which, of course, I could never live up to, which made me feel like shit. I learned that just because one "diet" worked for you for "X" amount of years doesn't mean that it will work for you forever. This was liberating for me. I learned to listen to my body and its innate intuition on what it needed instead of just living with a self-imposed label I had put on myself.

I had been craving eggs for about a year before I finally ate one, making me a non-vegan for the first time in about 12 years. I started having more energy and just feeling better in general.

Nowadays, I don't usually say I'm vegetarian, but rather, "plant-based." Not many people in this day and age can argue that eating more vegetables is better for you. Saying this also helps not to repel people. Over the years, I found that as soon as you say you're vegan, people immediately feel judged, get defensive, or run the other way.

Instead, I lead by example. I share my favorite veggie-full meals and inspire others to eat more nutrient-dense high-vibe foods.

Ok, so "High Vibe" to me, means living a life that will help you vibrate at a higher frequency. As spiritual beings, we will live a higher quality life if we fill our bellies and our lives with foods and activities that will support this instead of dragging us down.

As mentioned before, we all have something called a "morphogenic field." *lifefieldtechnique.com* explains it this way,

"The morphogenic field is one of the most important and least understood factors of influence within our society and our global culture. It is a field of energy containing a certain frequency or resonance, created by all living species that are both visible and invisible on planet Earth. All living species, human beings, animals, and plants have a consciousness and therefore an emotional field. Emotion and the energy connected to it is one of the most powerful forces of creation in existence.

Individually and collectively we constantly contribute to the development of our Universe with our thoughts and the emotional content behind them. Accessing fields of consciousness or morphogenic fields is as simple as resonance. For example, if you carry a high level of resonance for peace, the chances are that you will access peace easier and draw to you peaceful experiences. Likewise, if you have a high level of resonance for fear, the chances are equally good that you will find yourself tapping into more fear from that field and drawing validating and fearful experiences into your life.

If you have conscious awareness, you can keep yourself clear enough to be less influenced by negative morphogenic fields and choose to shift resonance to access fields that support your choices of higher awareness."

Basically, we all have an energy field around us and what we choose to do, think, say, and act will have an effect on this field as do the things we choose to or let surround us. It's up to us to consciously begin to keep our aura resonating where we want it to. We have come too far on our path to leave it up to chance or circumstance.

You're reading this book for a reason. You are ready to learn ways to keep lifted to the frequency that you choose because you need your light to be seen. It's not going to be seen, at least not how you want it to be seen, if you keep letting your morphogenic field get compromised by shitty food, shitty people, and shitty situations.

Some tips to start cleaning up your vibe:

- When possible, eat as much organic, local, seasonal produce as possible.
- Make veggies the staple of your diet, followed by fruits, nuts and seeds, lean proteins, whole grains, and healthy fats.
- Notice what friendships are draining you of your energy, making you feel bad about yourself or are only

one-sided. Start to distance yourself from these friendships as much as possible. As you begin to raise your vibe, they will usually fade away on their own.

- Commit to daily practices that will help protect your energy and also strengthen your energy such as meditation, yoga, chanting, working with healing crystals and essential oils, and doing things that you love.

- Practice gratitude and assloads of it. Every morning, list what you're grateful for and FEEL that gratitude. Do this any time throughout your day when you need a mental/emotional/spiritual reset.

- Stop watching things on T.V. that make you feel uneasy, helpless, hopeless, or depressed.

- Stop spending hours on social media, especially if it makes you feel like crap or disconnected from human connection. Only use it if you can find a way to help you feel uplifted, hopeful, and supported. Still, limit your time.

- Read more inspirational books or listen to the audio versions on the way to and from work.

- Listen to Abraham-Hicks audio recordings on YouTube.

- Pray.

- Talk to your angels, spirit guides, and ancestors daily.

- Start using oracle cards. I love Doreen Virtue's *Goddess Guidance Oracle Deck.*

Ways to make this more fun and/or easy:

- Find a local farm and see how you can support them. Do they have a CSA program?
- Have a cooking date with friends once per month and try out some new high vibe recipes each time.
- Find higher vibe friends by putting yourself out there
- Start taking some yoga classes and meet new people.
- Go to positive events at your local health food store or yoga studio.

Receiving and Our To-Do List

Momma, dearest, it's time to receive. Receive without guilt, receive without thinking you're not worth it. I talk with so many women who don't take time for themselves because they don't feel like they "should" or they should be doing yet one more thing for their kid's school, preparing a four-course dinner from scratch, cleaning the house, the list goes on and on.

This needs to stop.

When you are 90 years old, are you going to look back on your life and think, "Wow, I really wish I would have kept a cleaner house," or "If I would have only just said 'Yes' to being the head of that carpool"? I doubt it.

Chances are, you'll look back on your life and wish you would have enjoyed the little moments more. That time would have gone slower. You'll wish that you wouldn't have sweated the small stuff so much. You'll wish you would have enjoyed your body more.

You'll wish you had spent more time doing things that made you love life instead of things that just added to your list of things to do.

Really take some time to answer these questions. If you really want to get somewhere, journal about it.

1. What makes you think you NEED to do everything on your to-do list?
2. Why is your to-do list really so long?
3. Is there something from your past that is telling you that you are only good enough if you get all those things done?
4. Are you comparing yourself to other women who seem to have it all together?
5. Are you filling your time with busy work so you don't have to look at the real issues in your life?

Now, listen to me closely. The only person who can TRULY make us feel inadequate for not being superwoman is us. Sure, it may seem like it's coming from others but that's only because we allow it. They are only mirroring our own beliefs back to us.

Imagine being old and wrinkled. Having enjoyed a great life but wishing you'd done things differently. Really put yourself there. Visualize it. See it. Feel it.

Now grab your journal again and answer these questions:

1. What things would you have wanted to make more time for?

2. What people would you have wanted to spend more time with?

3. What grudges do you wish you'd let go of sooner?

4. Who do you wish you would have forgiven?

5. What do you wish you would have made time for every day?

6. How could you have better taken care of yourself?

7. What activities did you really love that you didn't make enough time for?

8. What things on your to-do list could you have let go of?

9. What things did you spend so much time worrying about or toiling over that, in the grand scheme of things, really didn't matter?

Really let it sink in your mind and your heart that this is your life to live. This is the only one you've got--with this body, this family, these exact experiences. Give yourself permission NOT to be perfect and remember

PERFECT DOES NOT EXIST!

This is one thing I've definitely learned over the years and it's certainly helped me cut myself more slack. "We do the best with what we have" is a great saying and one that comes in handy not only for us but also when we have situations with others where it's hard to see where they're coming from.

Yes, try your best but not at the cost of your own sanity. You MUST do things that serve *you*. You know how on airplanes they tell you to put your oxygen mask on before others? It's also true with self-care. It may seem selfish at first but the more you make that time for you, the better you'll be at managing your time more efficiently because you'll be better at putting things in perspective while also being way less stressed.

When you DON'T take time for you, you risk burnout, overwhelm, maybe even ending up in the hospital. Doesn't seem worth it, does it?

Along with more self-care and doing those things you love, start asking for help when you need it. If people say they are there for you and tell you they'd love to help, let them, dammit! You don't have to hold the weight of the world on your shoulders. There are no medals for that and there will always be One. More. Thing.

That's why our to-do lists seem never-ending. Because we let them get that way. Start having some tough conversations with yourself and start cutting out the shit that doesn't matter--the shit that is NOT enhancing your life--and start doing more of the things that do. Don't believe me? Try it for a month and see what happens. You'll see that the world doesn't buckle under the pressure of you not baking cookies for that fucking bake sale.

Open yourself up to receive and you'll receive more than you could have ever imagined. You'll open the pathway to Source. Intuition. Your Inner Guide. They will thank you for slowing your crazy ass down and enjoying the nectar of life. Finally.

How do you expect to have a connection to Spirit when you

don't sit quietly long enough to listen? Put down your phone. Close Facebook. Turn off the T.V.

- Go take a bath with a good book. Probably this one.
- Go for a walk. Alone. Without your phone.
- Unplug. MORE.
- Plant a vegetable or herb garden.
- Cook one soul-nourishing meal per week.
- Play with your kids or pets and don't rush it. Just let it happen.
- Color just for fun.
- Buy an expensive tea and enjoy it outside with some mellow jams.
- Get fresh flowers.
- Revamp or create a sacred space in a quiet space in your home.

Once you allow yourself to receive joy in your physical body, you allow your Soul to receive joy and abundance from Source. You are telling the Universe that you are worth it.

You *are* worth it. Every single one of us. You didn't do anything as a child to be unworthy. You didn't do anything as an idiot teenager to be unworthy and the fucked up shit you did yesterday? Still not unworthy.

You're a spirit having a human experience and fucking it up is what it's all about. When we do shit, that is fucked up or fucked up shit is done to us, we create shadows in our Soul. It's when we choose to shine our spiritual flashlight on these shadows that the magic happens. It may not always be fun and it may not always be pretty, but I can guaran-fucking-tee that it's totally, 100% worth it.

CHAPTER 8

Am I "Good" Enough?

One of the biggest struggles in my life is dealing with shame, regret, and guilt. As I previously mentioned, addiction has been in my life since my teen years, and just when I thought I was completely over it, it came back into my life leaving me questioning my authenticity as someone who puts myself out there in the "spiritual spotlight."

So many people think that being a yogi or someone on a spiritual path means that you have to be perfect. We already discussed that perfection doesn't exist. There is so much pressure in the yoga and spiritual world that we must maintain a certain type of lifestyle ALWAYS, otherwise, we don't feel good enough to call ourselves a yoga teacher or spiritual student.

This is ridiculous, and it's exactly the reason why I am sharing my story here, openly and honestly. Someone has to step forward and call bullshit. There are so many people that throw around the "authentic" word that I feel still aren't really showing us the other parts of their life that aren't perfect. In order for us to truly help others, we must start being real about our shit.

Now, I'm not going to spill all the gory details, but I want you to know that I certainly am not perfect and have given up trying to be. Some of my friends say that I shouldn't "hide who I really am" but I don't think that those times when I decide to check out of life for a bit with some beers is the "real me." It's the me that has some shit to deal with. It's the me that still needs to heal.

As yogis and spiritual sisters, we want to practice ahimsa, but what about when you think another yogi isn't living the life you think they should? Do you judge? Is that living without violence? I know I've done that in the past back when I thought the path was much more "cut and dry" but there's so much that we don't understand about life. How many times have you gone through a really hard time in your life, gotten through it, then, as a result, had a completely new and broader perspective on life? If you haven't yet had that, wait for it, it's coming--especially when you're doing this work and actually looking at the stuff that comes up. As we age, more and more realities are shown to us and sometimes it can be pretty darn uncomfortable. You must remember that other people are growing and going through these things, too, but probably in totally different ways.

When you judge someone else for how they live as being "wrong," it's time to take the mirror out and see why it bothers you so much. Do you see a little of them in you? Does it make something from your past come up?

It's not them, it's you.

A good friend of mine said that when we think we "slip up," we haven't fallen off our path but it's PART of the journey. I've realized that when I quit drinking and smoking with brute force a few years ago, I didn't actually do any of the work to heal why I was actually doing those things. I decided that when these things come back into my life, instead of feeling like a piece of crap, I will practice unconditional self-love. Sweeping it under the rug won't cut it. Oh, and if you get to go through that while going through a midlife crisis AND existential crisis like myself? All you can say is…

Touché universe. Touché.

I realize now that what I didn't heal was the part of me that loved myself less because of those things. I need to learn to love myself fully and completely. What I do now is talk to myself like I would my best friend. I would never judge her, and I would help to give her perspective. I know I am growing and that I am healing and it feels really good because I know the more I can love myself and shine the light on my shadow self, the more I can hold space for others. Writing this book has been part of my healing. It's bringing things up that I didn't even know were there.

The more darkness you find within yourself, the more potential you have for your light to shine. Expose it and deal with it when you're truly ready.

If you struggle with an addiction, be that playing games on your phone, shopping, scrolling social media, etc. ask yourself these questions:

1. Why was I trying to check out of my life?
2. What traumas from my past need to be dealt with so I can really move on?
3. Why am I not happy with who I really am?
4. Why do I not feel worthy?
5. What parts of me are unlovable?

And if you're at the point where you are hurting yourself or others, it's time to find help.

CHAPTER 9

Your Authentic Self

There are way too many people out there talking about "authenticity" who aren't really being fully real. Trust me, I get it. In this day and age of social media, it's easy to fall into the trap of only sharing the most amazing things from our lives and, for the most part, this is what I do. Not because I want to make myself look good but because I don't really complain in real life, let alone on Facebook. I'm a spreader of light, not of negativity but sometimes, to be that light, you have to get real and I do that by sharing bits and pieces of my journey that have been the hardest.

I don't do it for sympathy, if anything, I feel like a lot of people will like me less because of it. But I know that getting over what those people think is something I need to learn. (Because honestly, who gives a shit!) I share because I want everyone to know they have a place to go. I will never turn anyone away no matter how much they think they've messed up. I know that if I truly want the vibration of this planet to rise, we need more people out there living their truth, shining their light, and that light can only shine once it's no longer dimmed by self-doubt.

In order for this to happen, us brave ones need to show others that it's okay to be spiritual and NOT have all our shit together. This gives others hope that they, too, can begin or continue their spiritual journey even if they still do things they or others see as "not good enough." Why? Because we are learning and growing every day. Things will come up that you need to heal. If you're on this spiritual path and you asked for growth, it's not like you'll wake up one day and the world will be like, "Poof! You're magically wiser and more enlightened!" No. It's more like, "Okay, you really want it? Here you go then!"

Enter spiritual and emotional shit storm.

Some people may think that if you don't have all your shit together, you're not ready to teach yoga, but I think the opposite. Once you admit you don't have it together, you're ready to teach yoga. I've seen too many teachers pretend they are perfect only to fall a long way from the top. I feel it's much better to just start off at the bottom, admit that I'm just a lifelong student, but that I'm happy to be a guide for my students as long as they are happy to be their *own* Guru.

The thing is, yoga works for different people on different levels, at different times, in different ways. The true sign of a yogi is someone committed to becoming a better person, growing as a soul, and to understanding the world around them more. So, no matter what hangups a person has, if they are ready to grow, they are "good enough" to be a yogi or spiritual student.

Are you:

1. Committed to growing as a soul?
2. Committed to understanding the world around you more?

Yes? Congratulations! You're good enough to be a yogi or spiritual student!

Our journeys may not all look the same, but how we end up feeling about ourselves because of our "mistakes" may be very similar.

Practice picking yourself up out of these lower vibrations through activities such as:

- Journaling
- Dancing
- Singing
- Listening to audio recordings such as podcasts, audiobooks, or seminar recordings such as Abraham-Hicks on YouTube
- Crafting

- Walking in nature
- Meditating
- Playing with your kids or pets

Peeling Back the Layers

It's so silly. If any of my friends would come to me and tell me the same kind of things I feel shitty about, I would absolutely tell them they are a great person, that we all fall from that "ideal" version of ourselves. It is natural and actually part of the process. Just because we feel like we are backtracking doesn't mean that we aren't on our path anymore. We're learning and growing in new ways because of them.

The biggest thing that has helped me change my life is thinking about what kind of mother I want to be for my daughter but also, how I can continue to grow. I know I don't want to waste any more time, that's for sure. Spending too much time in lower levels of vibration wondering why you're such a loser definitely isn't going to help you make up for lost time!

Your Dream Life

The teachings of Abraham were a huge part of my spiritual understanding. I stumbled upon them after reading the first book that made me feel sane and not alone in my beliefs called *Conversations with God* by Neale Donald Walsch. I honestly can't remember how I found them because it was really before the days of searching for anything you can possibly imagine on the internet, but I'm so grateful I did.

They helped me to realize that everything is energy. As mentioned above, when you think certain thoughts, they will attract similar ones. That's why it's so important to try to get to a "higher flying disk" as they would say, to get yourself out of a lower vibration. If you can't jump all the way from a lower vibration thought to a much higher one, just work your way up slowly by thinking something just a little better.

Along with emotions attracting similar ones, our experiences are attracted by what we think. They are both just symptoms of what we have going on in our mind. I'm not saying to never feel the feels because I believe that is an important part of the process. We just can't get stuck there.

We have the ability to create the life of our dreams. Whatever we believe and see in our minds, we can manifest. I love working with the second and third chakras for this as the second chakra is where we create and the third is one of manifestation. More on chakras in the second half of this book.

So how do we do that?

By keeping your dreams in focus and by not letting your faith that it will happen fade. When we start to doubt ourselves, our dreams take a couple steps backward. When we don't let that pesky fear come in and instead just *know* it will happen, the dreams continue to move closer and closer into your reality.

This takes *practice*.

Most likely you won't be able to do this overnight because of all the limiting beliefs you've accepted as truths. That's okay. Be patient with yourself. It's like yoga off your mat. In yoga, you need to be content with where you are and this is no different. Every time you start feeling the fear instead of holding your vision, take a step back and get realigned. Throughout this book, you will learn many ways to do that.

I've seen the Law of Attraction prove true many times in my life. I've manifested amazing relationships both personally and professionally as well as money, which never hurts! I know when I'm not in alignment with my higher self, or with love, when it feels as though I'm moving upstream. It will feel like the more you TRY, the further things move away.

The key is to get into the flow. When things feel hard, that's because you're not listening to your inner guidance system. Take a break from what you're doing and reconnect to that part of you that believes in your ability to create. Trust me, it's there, it just has the tendency to get lost because of, well, life.

A great way to trick your mind is to create a vision board. Your mind doesn't know the difference between what is real and what you think. By looking at your vision daily and really sitting in what that would FEEL like, actually what it DOES feel like to have that life, you will bypass what IS and manifest your heart's desire. It may seem hard to believe now but dream BIG. The Universe doesn't distinguish between big or small dreams, it's only your beliefs around them that cause some more "attainable" things to manifest while the more lofty ideas won't come true or take longer.

If you 100% truly believed that you will get one million dollars this month, you will. But for most of us that doesn't seem likely.

Start small, test it out. Every time, throughout your day, you remember, think of something specific, maybe a yellow bird or a two dollar bill. Then watch for signs. Don't try too hard, just have it in your awareness to keep an eye out. It could show up in a magazine, on your morning walk, or even in a song.

For example, have you ever heard a new word then you see or hear it everywhere? Maybe you were just thinking of a song then you heard it on the radio. Have you ever thought of a friend that you haven't spoken to in months or years only to have them reach out to you soon after?

Yeah, that's the Law of Attraction (LOA).

I remember one of the first times I really focused on harnessing the energy of the Law of Attraction. After my husband and I took our first farming business course and decided we were going to leave the suburbs of Chicago, and his nice-paying job, to pursue our dream, I knew it was going to be tricky to sell our apartment at that time. Real estate was NOT selling and I knew I'd have to get creative at getting our place to sell, especially when there were similar condos for sale IN our own complex!

I decided I would use the LOA. I wrote out a pretend check, made it out to us, for the amount that we wanted to get for the condo. Each day, I would lay on the floor, envision it selling and us receiving that check from the buyers. I did this for a couple months.

It didn't happen overnight but we DID end up selling. We didn't get the amount we really wanted for it but we were one of the only ones that sold. Do you think we weren't happy about it? No way! There were still similar condos for sale a year after we sold ours!

This is the power of the Law of Attraction.

One of the other ways I like to use the LOA is by creating a vision board. This gives you something you can look at daily and get yourself into the mindset of actually HAVING what you desire. I look at it, close my eyes, and actually SEE myself enjoying that life. I like to use the word desire because it has a totally different energy than "want." When you "want" something, it has a desperation in it. When you desire something, it has a hopefulness in it. Big difference.

You can create a vision board on a sheet of poster board by cutting out images from magazines or printed out from the internet and glued to it. Make it pretty! Another way to create a vision board is to download the Hay House Vision Board app. That way you always have it with you! You can even create different vision boards for different areas of your life. Maybe you're writing a book and you have a vision for the outcome. Get it on paper! Make it visual. Trick your mind into believing you already have these things and it will come WAY faster than if you are always depressed because you don't have them.

The other thing you MUST have is gratitude. Have gratitude for EVERYTHING you love in your life. Throughout your day, make lists of all you are grateful for and FEEL that gratitude. If this is hard for you, start small. Have gratitude for your bed, your children, your dog. When you get in this mindset, the Universe has no choice but to bring you more of the same vibration.

CHAPTER 10

Gratitude Heals

"You must have gratitude. Have it for everything in your life that you love. The Universe will hear you and it has no choice but to bring you more of the same."
-- Crystal Gray

There's really nothing more powerful than that of being grateful. Over the years, I've learned this from many spiritual teachers but my main source of spiritual knowledge would have to be the teachings of Abraham from Esther and Jerry Hicks.

When I am dealing with overwhelming feelings of anxiety,

despair, or any other negative emotion, one of my favorite things to do is to listen to one of the audio recordings on YouTube. It's my go-to to change how I am feeling and to "reset" for my day.

I've learned from them that when you focus on being grateful or satisfied, there isn't room for negative emotions about something else. Physical symptoms in the body show up because of unresolved emotions that you are still holding onto. We don't have to spend loads of time going into our past and keep reliving or spending time IN this emotion, rather, we can release it and take its power away by focusing on what we are grateful for and what makes us feel satisfied.

A powerful exercise I use every morning to ensure I start my day on the best note possible is gratitude journaling. I've recently begun switching it up with things that make me feel satisfied. They're pretty closely related but I feel that by getting down to even smaller, often overlooked things, that make your life a little easier or more pleasurable can be an easier task than feeling gratitude. It's a good place to start.

When practicing gratitude, you can even write about what you are grateful for that hasn't happened yet. I know that may sound a little crazy but our minds don't know the differences between what has happened and what hasn't. It only goes by images. So if you are FEELING gratitude for those things you are desiring, then the Universe has no choice but to bring it to you.

I like to combine my two gratitude lists into one and, while writing what I DO have that I'm grateful for, I sprinkle in things that I desire to manifest and act as though they've already come to me! You can do this same trick with a vision board. Usually, those are full of things we desire, but how would it change the energy if you sprinkled in things you already HAVE in your life that make you feel gratitude? Gratitude is the magical emotion that will pull it all together and help you weave your dream life into being.

Another easy way to fit more gratitude or feelings of satisfaction in your day, as well as to turn around a bad mood, is to just start to make a mental list of everything you see that you're grateful for today. The sun shining, the fresh air you are lucky enough to breathe, the flowers blooming, the snow melting, the smell of homemade lasagna baking in the oven, anything that brings you joy at this moment, show some gratitude for it! Name it, say it out loud, do a little dance and see how you start to appreciate all the little joys of life.

What could be better than slowing time down and enjoying every moment even more?

The Present Moment

All we really have is the present moment. If we can't find happiness now, will we really have it when our "dream life" is here? Will we even recognize when it is here? It seems like so many people are waiting for the perfect job, to lose 30 pounds, to reach retirement, or to find the right partner to be happy. We think THEN everything will be great, and we'll magically find the peace in life we are looking for. But how many times have you reached that goal only to find that you immediately move on to the next life goal? You don't even take time to relish what you've achieved. Trust me, I've fallen into this trap, too.

I've learned that we MUST take the time to enjoy where we're at, what we've done, and how far we've come. If we only keep moving toward the next big thing, once we get there, we'll feel empty. The key is in the present moment.

Always striving for more will leave you feeling lost and unfulfilled. In order to end this cycle, you have to find gratitude for every day. You have to learn how to enjoy what you have and who you are RIGHT NOW. This is a practice. You can't keep going through life feeling that way or it will pass you by.

By being in the present moment, you will slow down time.

Some ways you can do this are to:

1. Set an intention for your day and come back to it often throughout the day. You can set a reminder on your phone for every hour or two, then take a moment to close your eyes and get back in tune with that intention.

2. Have a gratitude practice throughout the day. Start the morning with five minutes of closing your eyes and FEELING gratitude. You'll know when you reach that point. Usually, when I reach it, my eyes tear up a bit. Think about things that truly make you feel grateful to be alive.

3. Wake up five to ten minutes early, close your eyes, breathe deeply, and do something called light sourcing (I learned this from one of Rebecca Campbell's books). Sit up tall and envision and white healing light above you, coming from whatever you see as God, Source, the Universe, even Mother Nature. Let that

light flow into you from the crown of your head all the way down to the base of your body, filling every fiber of your being with healing love and light.

4. See the learning in all situations. Instead of making it get you way off track and make you have a terrible day, take a step back and see what you can learn from it. This can really change your perspective and stop you from going into a dark place.

5. Practice yoga. The more you do these things on your mat, the easier it is to practice off your mat.

CHAPTER 11

Birds of a Feather Flock Together

> *"You are the average of the five people you spend the most time with."*
> **-- Jim Rohn**

Take a moment to think about who you spend the most time with. Are they positive people? Are they moving toward the same things in life that you are? Are they on the same path?

If the answer to these questions is "no," then you have some work to do. When we are surrounded by people that aren't where we are trying to "go" in life, the chances that you'll be able to get to that place in your life are greatly reduced.

Think about it. When you surround yourself with people that make you feel bad about yourself, don't inspire you, make fun of your dreams, or tell you that you can't do something, how does it make you feel? Does it give you the confidence to go out there and work toward your dream life or does it make you just settle for what's already in front of you?

Maybe they don't do anything this blatantly obvious. They could just be negative people in general, complainers, or lazy. Perhaps they just don't see the world the way you do. In any case, it's not helping you to reach your full potential.

What could your life be like if you, instead, started hanging around those who inspired you? That made you work harder? That showed you the kind of life you *could* have if only you started doing some inner work? Even if you didn't reach any huge dreams, wouldn't just feeling better about yourself and the world be worth it to change who you let be a huge part of your life?

I'm not saying to go out and completely stop being around these people. That might be difficult and confusing to yourself and them. The best way, in my experience, is to start doing the inner work on yourself first, then your outer world will begin to fall into place. When we start to shift, anything that doesn't vibrate at that same level will begin to fall away. It's just how the Universe works.

This works in your advantage and can work against you, too. If you start being more negative by complaining or dwelling on the not-so-good parts of your life or the world in which we live, you will then attract others who feel the same, and once you start commiserating with them, the worse it will get.

Like attracts like.

So how can you start actively letting go of those who are dragging you down? The first thing you can do, especially if you still have to be around them, is to really get centered before you spend time with them. Get into alignment with who YOU are.

Close your eyes, take some deep breaths, and visualize surrounding yourself with a protective, loving, white light or energy. Continue until you feel peaceful and confident.

Know that when you get around people that bother you, it's really not them . . . I know, hard to believe. It's actually your reaction to the situation. It's easy to point the finger. It takes work to turn it back onto ourselves but if you want to grow and evolve, this is the work that needs to be done.

Keep this in mind when you must be in the presence of people that make you feel bad in some way. Continue moving forward and getting yourself into alignment and the people and situations that made you feel that way will either start to fade away or shift in some way to where it just doesn't bother you anymore.

Another thing that helps me when dealing with difficult people is to remember that we are all doing the best we can with what we have. We all grow up and learn different behaviors and beliefs. These things can make seeing eye-to-eye challenging. It's best not to judge. Instead, ponder why it bothers you, use it for your own spiritual growth and move on. Don't hold it against them. Instead, show gratitude for the lessons it brought you. This shift in mindset will save you a lot of heartache!

As the old begins to fade away, start watching for people that inspire you. Some ways to do this:

- Join Facebook groups with similar interests
- Join local meetups that focus on topics that you're excited about
- Join adult sports leagues
- Go to more yoga classes and events at yoga studios
- Find local spiritual groups
- Raise your vibration by reading self-help books (such as this one), practicing yoga and meditation, and eating more nourishing foods
- Stop complaining
- Stop gossiping
- Stop dwelling on the negative
- Practice affirmations

Remember that this, along with many other ideas in this book, is a practice. It isn't going to happen overnight and that's okay. Take your time and enjoy the process.

"Change only happens in the present moment. The past is already done. The future is just energy and intention."
— Kino MacGregor

CHAPTER 12

But Everyone Else Has Their Shit Together!

When I ask women what stresses them out the most, it usually has something to do with their to-do list, which never seems to get done. We always feel like we are falling short and therefore aren't good enough and don't measure up to what we think we "should" be getting done on a daily basis while also comparing ourselves to all the "perfect" women out there that have all their shit together.

I'm here to tell you that the women that you think have all their ducks in a row…

They Don't!

They can act like they do. They can make it look like it on social media. They can do nothing at ALL, but your perception leads you to believe that they have no worries, and they are so fucking lucky because you got dealt a bad hand and have it so much worse and it's not fair because you're a good person and how can they look like that when they have five kids and I only have one and I look like this and, and, and…

Stop it.

Just stop.

If anyone had all their shit together, they'd have reached enlightenment. They'd be done with their work here on Earth. The thing you need to realize is that it's all about accepting what has been put on your path and dealing with it with grace. Once you can do this, you will feel like superwoman.

Let me reiterate. It's not about not HAVING issues. It's about how you react to them.

We all have challenges on our path; this is life, after all. We're here to learn, to grow. So many times we pray for the qualities or the life we want, but when the Universe gives us those opportunities that will help us grow, we complain and get all victim-y about it. How will you learn patience if you're not in situations that will help you practice it? How will you learn how to stop comparing yourself to others that seem to have it all if you don't get the chance to do it?

Instead of getting mad at the world, let's find gratitude for Source giving us the opportunity to grow. What's the alternative? Complain, gossip, and get yourself to the bottom of a really nice downward spiral? Well, that sounds fun, too, but it's up to you.

Just kidding, of course. But that is a familiar place to be so it's easy for us to slip back into it over and over. Just like yoga, this is another practice. It may not be fun or easy, but in the long run, you will be happier, more content and at peace with your life.

Stop Hating on Your Body

So many women spend so much of their day wishing their bodies were different. They wish it were thinner, prettier, younger, more capable, the list goes on and on. We end up hating and despising our bodies for not being what we want. I really feel that when the majority of women are focused upon these high standards that are not real and definitely not the norm, we are wasting valuable time and energy that could be spent making a difference in the world.

You could be spending your time, thoughts, and energy thinking of ways to make a difference, of ways to be more in the present moment, or being more grateful and appreciative for what your body does for you.

I strongly believe that our bodies give back to us whatever resonates with the thoughts we are thinking about it. If you truly love your body, are grateful and appreciative of the things it CAN do for you, and what it does for you every day without even having to ask, you will change your life. Your body will begin to be the body you've always wanted. Either your perspective will change, not caring about the stretch marks (that are perfectly natural and came about from the miraculous act of CREATING a child INSIDE of your own body), or your body will actually change.

You will start to feel better when you focus on the things you

ARE grateful for instead of the things you hate your body for.

Try it for just 21 days and see what happens. Every time you start to think a negative thought about your body--shame, guilt, unworthiness, and the like, immediately catch yourself, stop that thought dead in its tracks, and change it to something you are GRATEFUL for. If this is hard, think of something that just makes you satisfied. Something that just allows you to FREAKING LIVE. The fact that you can breathe, that you can smell flowers blooming or bread baking, that you can see your children or grandchildren, that you can laugh and hear the laughter of others.

I know many of us can feel betrayed by our bodies if we are suffering from chronic pain or other ailments. It's not a welcome thought that we may have caused this within our bodies because of our thoughts. You might say, "I wouldn't have brought on cancer, I don't want it." And while that may be true, always thinking, "I don't want cancer, I don't want cancer, I don't want cancer" will most likely end up bringing it to you. It is law and it's how the Universe works.

There are schools of thought that say there are other reasons we may get dis-ease or are born with dis-ease. It could be from karma from past lives or something your soul signed up for before coming into this body so that you could learn an important lesson for your soul's growth or help others learn from you to help their souls grow. I think it could also be from your body holding onto emotions in certain parts of the body, "clogging" it up in a way.

No matter the reason, I think we have the power to heal our bodies fully. When we become empowered with the idea that we can change how our bodies feel, look, or what they are capable of --

miracles can happen.

And it all starts in the mind.

An Ode to Your Body

Every moment you have the choice to choose a good-feeling thought or a bad-feeling thought.

A lot of these bad feeling thoughts may be directed at your body for not being thin enough, pretty enough, young enough, or capable enough. The list goes on.

Our poor bodies. They do so much for us, yet how do we treat them in return?

How often do you show appreciation for your body?

After all, they just:

Breathe for us
Laugh for us
Feel pleasure for us
Hear music for us
Cry for us
Birth human beings or ideas for us
Carry us through this thing called life.

It's the only thing with us for our entire journey.

It is your soul's vehicle. Your partner. Your friend.

It's time to stop wondering what your body "should" be doing for you and start thinking about what you can do for *it*.

Some ways to start showing more gratitude and appreciation for your body:

- Rewiring your negative thoughts
- Looking in the mirror daily and saying, "I love you"
- Touching each part of your body with appreciation and telling it that you love it and appreciate it (eventually, you'll mean it)
- Practice a type of yoga that makes you feel good about yourself
- Meditate
- Journal about all the thoughts that come up during the day that tell you your body isn't good enough
- Dance like no one is watching and for extra credit, do it sensually
- Have more pleasurable encounters with a partner or yourself
- Eat nourishing, fresh, whole foods, smoothies, or juices
- When you do treat yourself, do it without guilt
- Move your body more
- Get out in nature
- Donate time to helping others with limitations
- Start telling yourself the same things you'd tell your daughter or an important young woman in your life about HER body

- Spend time with fun and uplifting women that don't focus on appearance or weight constantly

I used to spend so much time hating on my body. I'd count every single calorie that went into my body. I'd obsess over the scale. I'd exercise daily and I definitely wasn't enjoying it, it was a MUST in order to look the way I thought I should, though I never did look the way I wanted. This lasted throughout high school and came about after I started taking the birth control pill.

Before I started taking "the pill" I was thin and beautiful--I was 14. When I turned 15, I got on the pill to regulate my periods even though they weren't even that crazy to begin with. I just had no idea how to track them and didn't want to be surprised when they came. It was just the thing to do. Needless to say, I gained about 20-30 pounds over the next couple of years, going from around 115 to 145.

I got so much bullying from the boys and girls in my school about being "fat." This did nothing for my self-esteem, let me tell you. From then on until my late 20's, I struggled with my weight, even though it did settle to 130-135 after I got off the pill but it was still never good enough.

Once I got serious with my yoga practice, I started seeing my body as something capable, strong, and flexible. Something that could do so much of what was asked of it and then some. I started to naturally want to eat more foods that would support it and let go of things that didn't support it or make it feel good. When you drink a six or--who am I kidding--a twelve pack of beer and smoke a pack of cigarettes the night before, you aren't going to get as much out of your yoga practice had you skipped them and spent that time preparing a healthy meal instead.

For a long time, I balanced out my bad habits with as many good habits as possible. I yo-yo'd for years, drinking and smoking for a couple months then quitting for a whole month to only go back to it after all that hard work of quitting. It was a vicious cycle.

But the thing about yoga is that if you stay with it, even when all the shit comes up that you don't want to look at, it WILL change your life. It WILL lead to other things that will also change your life. It made me open my eyes to the importance of daily meditation, of connecting to my Intuition, of surrendering to Source.

The key is to stick with it. When you do, your life will look completely different from just one year before.

Some tips to stick with it:

1. Know that it won't always be roses and sunshine, shit is GOING to come up.
2. When this shit DOES come up, look at it. Don't run away from it. Journal about it, talk about it, go to therapy, get energy healing--just DEAL with the stuff.
3. Being committed doesn't mean you have to do an hour-long power yoga class every day. It means doing some form of yoga daily, some days, this might be 20 minutes of meditation, others, it might be a 15-minute gentle practice or an hour-long vinyasa class. Do what your body, mind, emotions, and spirit need today.
4. Check in daily to SEE what you need. I always start my day with meditation which I consider a huge part of my yoga practice. If I do an asana or physical practice that day, too, well then that's

just icing on the cake. After my meditation, I am better prepared to tune into my Intuition and feel what I need that day in regard to a physical practice. Maybe I'll just dance my ass off and sing at the top of my lungs while I'm getting ready for my day. Whatever floats your boat, as long as it gets you into alignment.

5. Find a group of like-minded women that will inspire you and support you in your growth and on this journey. A lot of people won't understand and will want you to stay small because it brings up fear in THEM. So find your tribe. You can join our free tribe by going to our website.

www.yogagoddessacademy.com

6. Don't make this another thing you HAVE to do. Make it something that is non-negotiable because you MATTER and you DESERVE it and you are WORTHY of self-care. Put it in your calendar now.

7. Start SMALL. Does meditation scare or bore the shit out of you? Start with just three minutes but do it EVERY day. Just sit up in bed BEFORE looking at your phone, set the timer for three minutes and go for it. I love to use the Insight Timer app for this. When you have more time, you could do a meditation from the Yoga Goddess Academy.

8. It's okay if other people don't understand what you're doing. You can keep it to yourself or you can share with those who will be supportive in your growth.

9. Some relationships will naturally fall away that don't resonate at the place where you're vibing now. That's okay. Some relationships will have to grow and expand to match where you are and you need to be patient with them and let them evolve.

10. A new you means others will need some time to get used to and re-adjust to your newfound confidence and passion. And that's okay, too. Allow them that time but also talk calmly about what you're going through and why this is important to you. That you love them and want to grow together, not apart.

11. Ask how you can better support those in your life that you love and watch how the Universe helps to bring you more support in your journey.

12. When life throws you a curveball, analyze it instead of reacting to it.

13. Be in the present moment more so that you can slow down and enjoy the good stuff more often.

14. Relax. There is no destination, no endpoint. Enjoy the path, every step of the way. That's the whole reason why we're here, after all.

Mirroring

One of the best things we can do to help ourselves grow is to stop blaming others, our current situations, and our past for anything that is going wrong in our life. I see so many people blaming others for their own unhappiness. If someone says something rude to you in a harsh tone, instead of immediately just going the easy route and thinking, "Damn, she's a bitch," take that opportunity to grow and look at yourself. I'm not saying everyone should just be walking around saying bitchy things, but I AM saying that if those of us who are on the receiving end of things like this would just take a moment to step back instead of immediately reacting, we'd have a lot less stress in our lives.

Through my many years of being a yoga teacher, I have seen this amplified in the classroom. In a yoga class, students are releasing old energy that has been stuck in their body--physical or auric body--and when they aren't ready to look at their junk, guess where it goes? Yep, right on the teacher. I've had a few difficult students that I knew this was happening with, yet something kept them coming back. I have no doubt I learned just as much, if not more, from the situation than they did because I was willing to take it as a learning experience instead of judging them for their actions.

This might just sound like I AM actually a bitch and blaming others for seeing me in my true light. I'm not going to argue that there are some people that truly feel that way about me. But I am wise enough to finally realize that others' opinions of me DO NOT DEFINE ME.

Do you know how liberating this is? When you are constantly stuck in the world of, "I hope I didn't piss them off," "I hope they like me," or "I hope they don't think I'm a bitch," you are exactly that--stuck. I'm not saying a healthy dose of watching your boundaries isn't good but when this is more important than how YOU see yourself and the person you KNOW yourself to be, then that's a problem.

You HAVE to love yourself truly, unconditionally, and if you don't fit into someone else's mold of how a person should be, then that just has to be okay. You can't spend your life trying to fit into that box. Check in with yourself and make sure you are coming from a place of love, service, and alignment rather than fear, greed, and ego. If you find you were coming from a lower vibration then you need to look in the mirror and see what's true and let the rest go.

Mirroring isn't always about talking yourself off a ledge because of how others behave, it's, more importantly, a spiritual tool for you to use to assess situations so you can learn and grow from them instead of becoming incapacitated by them.

Ways we can use the "mirroring tool" in our daily life:

- See the people in our life that aggravate us the most as our biggest teachers
- When you see things within others that you don't like, look to see if you have some of those same qualities within yourself that you aren't proud of
- Notice if situations or other people that bother you may be bringing up stuck or repressed emotions from your past

See the people in our life that aggravate us the most as our biggest teachers.

This may be really difficult to do at first, but over time, you will be grateful for these experiences that actually do serve you, though they may bug the crap out of you! They do take the effort to learn from. It may be easier to pass it off as being the other person's shortcoming but, deep down, if you look hard enough, there will be something for you to uncover.

I have found that this really does get easier over time. Whereas it used to take me a few days to a week or longer to sit with it, meditate on it, and sometimes, talk it out, now I might be able to figure it out in one or two days. I do think it has something to do with being able to be grateful for whatever the situation is trying to teach or show me rather than react to it by getting super fired up about it or blaming others.

This is most definitely a practice. This is what I call taking my yoga "off the mat."

When you see things within others that you don't like, look to see if you have some of those same qualities within yourself that you aren't proud of.

This may be the learning experience that I mentioned above. Most likely, this is what other people's "negative" behavior will show you. Have you ever seen someone be in a bad relationship only to get out of it and get into another one just like it? It may have even happened to you!

It's like with me teaching yoga. Until I was able to be grateful for my difficult students and actually see it as a learning experience for myself was I able to free myself of the relationship. Even if you do miraculously free yourself from that person, if you haven't learned what you needed to learn from it, you'll most likely attract the same type of person into your experience again. So you might as well just deal with it now!

Notice if situations or other people that bother you are actually bringing up stuck or repressed emotions from your past.

If you can't figure out why in the heck this person or situation is bothering you so much, it could be some old energy that needs to be looked at and let go of. What from your past feels similar to the way you feel now? Who or what made you feel that way?

Ways to work through the mirroring lesson:

- Don't react!
- Take time to step back and reflect
- Journal
- Meditate
- Pray
- Ask for guidance or signs from your Angels, spirit guides, or ancestors
- Pull oracle cards
- Breathe

When we take the time to effectively look at and understand these mirrors, we can then be more of a clear channel. When we don't manage how we react to these mirrors, we're letting not only our ego, but our old wounds run the show. These wounds can manifest in many ways: addictions, control issues, making others feel less than, blaming, to name a few.

As I've already mentioned, I am nowhere near perfect. I'm not a saint, I'm not the most "pure" yogi and probably never will be, but I DO commit to cleansing myself emotionally and spiritually by addressing these issues so that I can be as much of a clear channel for the Divine as possible. It's so important to remain humble and it can be very healing to show your flaws. It's my philosophy that it's better to show your flaws before people find out about them. Be honest about them and commit to truthfully looking at them, so they can no longer control your life. Bring them up and out of the shadows and your life will change in miraculous ways.

Other people's opinions

Fuck 'em.

No, but seriously, you have to stop caring what other people think. This is something that I find may come with age, but why wait until you're older to stop letting it hold you back? That's ALL it does. Sure, you may stay in certain peoples' good graces but how much does that really matter? Is that why you came here? To please others? I highly doubt it and if you really dig deep and ask your Spirit, I think you'll find the same.

I spent so many years shaming myself and going further and further down into a shame spiral because I'd "screw up" now and then but who decides what "screwing up" even is? For fuck's sake, most likely it was PART of your path, and here you are, beating yourself up over it rather than accepting it so that you can learn and grow from it. Think how much further along you'd be in your life if that's how you handled most situations instead of feeling like a piece of crap because of it?

We can't make everyone happy and there is NO point in trying. You have this one lifetime here in this body with these exact skills and experiences and you HAVE to make it count. Find friends who are on this same level--who don't judge you, who lift you up and inspire you to be more. It always helps to have people in your corner that you can turn to because they'll help you realize that even if others do say things about your choices, it's THEIR shit that's coming up, their mirrors that are being reflected, NOT yours. If they have a problem with it, it's just that--THEIR problem.

Now, if you let THEIR problem become yours, then you're making it your problem and don't you have enough shit to think about already without adding that to your plate? You're a spiritual warrior now, you're on a mission to dig this stuff up and look at it so you can change your life. You're ready to grow and awaken and you KNOW that worrying about others' opinions of you is the last thing that's going to help you get there.

I can't imagine all the time I've wasted and all the accomplishments I haven't reached yet because of my limiting beliefs. I know there are people who will disagree with me, who will think I'm not as good as them because of what I say and what I've done, but chances are, that I wouldn't really want to be around them anyway because they're too hung up on judgments, and they aren't my kind of peeps.

Well, guess what, I'm DONE with that shit. I'm done living small because of those fears of not being good enough. I've fucked up and I'm not perfect and I'm the first to say it. You with me? Admitting that is so freeing because then you're beating them to the punch. If you have already admitted it, then there's nothing to be scared of. Let's do this.

If you're wondering HOW to do this, it's like all the other practices in this book. It takes practice and awareness. Every time you start thinking those nasty thoughts you have to take a step back, acknowledge them, look at them, see where they came from, tell yourself how limiting it is to think that way, then move forward. The thoughts will keep coming, but you will build up the skills and it will get easier and easier. The key here is to keep going.

Releasing Attachment Ritual Prayer

Calling upon Archangel Michael to help release
the cords that are negative, holding me back, and keeping
me from stepping into who I truly am meant to be--my
FULLEST self.

I release any and all attachments to others.

My self-worth comes from within.

Unconditional love comes from within.

I heal my heart from these wounds, attachments, and cords.

I open the front and back of my heart to be healed.

I release relationships and cords that I carry due to obligation or
devotion.

I set myself free.

Unconditional love comes from within.

My self-worth comes from within.

Confidence comes from within.

True support comes from within.

Stop looking for these things outside of you.

You have everything you are currently seeking OUTSIDE of you--INSIDE of you already.

Once you know this, you are liberated, you are set free.

You will have Heaven on Earth.

You are a child of God.
You are He and He is She.

You are Divine.

You are magnificent.

You hold the keys to all the mysteries of the Universe.

Believe it. Now is YOUR time.

You. The Magnificent. You. The Goddess.

Helping Others Shine

Once you start shining more brightly, others may start coming to you to help them figure out how to turn on their light. This can be very challenging for you, especially when it's so easy to let our ego take the reins and spout off advice that is from our personal experience.

Instead of giving the power to your ego, use these tips to really help your friend find their way.

Listen. Truly listen. Try not to rush and give advice based on your history, your experience, your past. Every soul is unique. We have different things to learn so giving advice based on your life is biased and may not be what's best for them.

Ask questions. As a coach and yoga teacher trainer, I know the power of asking questions. By doing this, you help *them* come up with the answers that are best for them. You help them dig deep and get connected to *their* truth.

Listen more. You don't have to be their Guru. They are their own Guru. You are just helping them to remember. We are all on the same level though sometimes we forget.

Give *them* the power. Help them to turn on their light instead of continually depending on you to do it for them.

This may not make your ego happy but this is our true gift. The world is shifting and this is one of the amazing ways that you can be an integral part of making this happen. Thank you, for leading the way.

Crises

Something that has been coming up for me lately is thoughts of identity. When I'm dealing with anxiety that is bubbling up from doing some deeper work, I can get stuck in the muck of negative thinking. I think things like, "Who am I to be a yoga teacher?" or "Who am I to share my ideas on these spiritual subjects?" Also, feelings of, "Why am I even doing this in the first place?" or "What's the point?"

I put so much pressure on myself to be successful, to come far from where I once was, that I get myself lost in a sea of self-doubt. When these feelings come up, I have to think about WHY they are coming up and actually DEAL with them instead of sweeping them under the rug.

I feel like so much of the time we just sweep the unpleasant subjects under the rug. When we do this, though, we're not really healing anything, we're just suppressing it. Sometimes this is necessary because we're not yet mentally or spiritually equipped to deal with it in a meaningful way. It might not be for a while but when you become aware of these things lurking in the shadows, that's when it's time to shine the light on them. Be patient with the process.

When you feel lost in your life and not sure what your purpose is, know that you're not alone. In fact, it's an actual "thing." Wikipedia says that:

"An existential crisis is often provoked by a significant event in the person's life—psychological trauma, marriage, separation, major loss, the death of a loved one, a life-threatening experience, a new love partner, psychoactive drug use, adult children leaving home, reaching a personally significant age (turning 16, turning 40, etc.), etc. Usually, it provokes the sufferer's introspection about personal mortality, thus revealing the psychological repression of said awareness.

An existential crisis may stem from one's new perception of life and existence.

Wikipedia also states that many things can spur this type of crisis. Some of them are:

A new-found grasp or appreciation of one's mortality, perhaps following a diagnosis of a major health concern such as a terminal illness

Believing that one's life has no purpose o external meaning

Searching for the meaning of life

Shattering of one's sense of reality, or how the world is

An extremely pleasurable or hurtful experience that leaves one seeking meaning

Realizing that the Universe is more complex, mysterious, larger, and beyond current human understanding;"

You may have been feeling this way but never put words to it. It really is hard to find the words that capture how you feel. I believe that this is all part of the process, part of our path, especially the spiritual path. We have to face the situation so that we can move forward with greater meaning. Long story short:

It's time to stop fucking around.

You are your Own Guru

Putting all your faith in a guru will leave you lost when they fall. Trust me, I've been there, more than once. I wasn't hurt because I learned they weren't perfect. I was hurt because I found out they weren't who I thought they were, which is WAY worse. Again, this is why I lay all my chips on the table. I want my students to know that I'm not perfect, I still fuck up, and that I am only a guide-- someone who has been through some stuff. I am just a person who is willing to talk about it in order to help others know they aren't alone.

I am no one's guru. YOU are your own Guru and don't let anyone take that away from you. You are here living YOUR life, not someone else's. Yes, you can take others' viewpoints into consideration but, no matter what, no one has walked in the shoes you've walked in. We've all been through trauma, we've all been scarred. They may not look the same, but we've all made it to where we are today because we're tough. We know we are meant to be here, but sometimes, we forget why.

And that's okay! We may be in "alignment" for many years, then all of a sudden, due to working on deep issues that need to come up or maybe it's because of some huge astrological event, we become a bit unhinged, we remember we're human. No matter the cause, we all fall sometimes. We HAVE to, or we wouldn't have that contrast. If we didn't have that contrast, we wouldn't be able to truly appreciate when we ARE in alignment.

If more teachers admitted to this, then I think we'd do a better job at helping others see that you don't have to fit into any certain mold to be a yogi or spiritual seeker. You just have to be human AND to want it, of course.

When you find out your teacher isn't at all who you thought they were, it is pretty disheartening. You may lose your faith in what you had been so committed to practicing. You may lose your way. This is why we mustn't put all our eggs in one teacher's cart. This is why we MUST be our own Guru and take what others say as an idea. See if that idea fits with your beliefs, and if not, either see if this idea can challenge you and help you grow, or let it go.

There's no value in being dogmatic. Whether we like it or not, we don't know everything. We can have IDEAS on things but there's just no way to know. When someone says they DO know how things are, for sure, 100%, not just this-is-what-I-believe-but-you-make-your-own-decision, I run the other way.

This is a new era, one where we are finally able to start speaking out, to step more into our own energy and connect to the Divine Feminine energy on this planet. The world needs to shine YOUR light, YOUR gifts, YOUR soul, not someone else's idea of what that should look like.

You are a Guru for the person that matters most to you in this lifetime. YOU. Don't let her down.

CHAPTER 13

What's Next?

So now that you are ready to stop fucking around by playing small, what's next?

Well, it's time to get real and do some soul-searching. It's time to find meaning, purpose, and vision for your life; Something that will make you jump out of bed in the morning.

When you have a purpose you feel:

Excited

Inspired

Joyful

Exuberant

Peaceful

Driven

And when you're confident with your purpose, you know that there is no need for competition with others. Your mission is specific to you, no two are alike and, therefore, there is no reason to compare yourself to others or to try to climb over others to get to the top.

When you realize that there is enough to go around, you are released from SO much unneeded stress. But your purpose can sometimes be a difficult thing to find, especially when you're so used to listening to the outside world instead of your own inner guidance system, your Intuition.

We can easily be persuaded into believing that our purpose is to make money to support our family, to grow up and be a doctor (because our father was one), to get married and have children (because that's what women do)--the list goes on. But these things aren't our purpose unless we CHOOSE for them to be. This choice has to come from our Spirit, not from those around us and not from a place of fear. When we let other people's expectations play into what we do with our life, we are disconnecting ourselves from Source.

Usually, this happens early in life and especially when going into college. We're so young that most of us have NO idea what we want to do with our lives, so we either ask for other's opinions or, more than likely, they just give them to us. We start doing what we THINK we should do instead of what we FEEL we should do. We must give our children space and time to feel for themselves. This isn't easy as parents or as loving adults because we don't want them to "mess up" their life, but we have to remember that it's part of the process.

If you look back on your life, you probably see that you "messed up" a good amount of times and hopefully, by now, you are well-adjusted enough to realize that all those experiences helped shape who you are now and actually gave your life more meaning in one way or another. Maybe not the fuck-up itself but what it led to. Teach the young ones around you instead to listen to their own inner guidance system and lead by example. Show them that you have faith in them, so they can have faith in them, too. Think about how our world could be different if this is what we taught the younger generations.

During your life, you will find that you may have different purposes at different times. When you have a brand-new baby, for example, your purpose is to keep that child happy and alive. But as that child grows, you start to have more freedom to do more outside of your role of being a mother.

In college, your purpose may be to learn as much as you can so you can do well in your career after you graduate. If you're already in a job, your purpose may be to help as many people as possible. This doesn't mean you have to be a doctor and save people's lives. This could mean that you want to help people see the bright side of things. You can do THAT in ANY job. The key is to find happiness wherever you are right NOW. Even if you don't LOVE your job, find things about it that make you grateful such as the money it brings into your life to allow you to pay bills for things like electricity that keeps you warm on cold nights.

Remember, when you are grateful, you will get more of those things that make you grateful. More of those positive aspects will be delivered to you. This could be in a promotion or in a new job offer. You never know how the Universe will provide it, you just have to have faith that it will. This will help you get closer and closer to discovering your purpose because you will be in a place of receiving Divine Guidance and miracles.

Begin leaning into those things that make you happy, that make you feel joy or any feeling that resonates on the same frequency of love. This will be your guiding force and it will NEVER steer you in the wrong direction. Just like yoga, it is a practice. It will get easier and easier but may be a little tricky in the beginning. Don't let this dissuade you from moving forward. It may not be the easy road but it is the road to happiness and inner peace, and I'd say those things are well worth the effort. I'm sure you know some of those people that choose to remain stuck. Heck, that person may be you or has been you in the past.

You must quit blaming others and situations for your life not turning out how you want it to; You MUST take responsibility.

Once you do this, things will get easier. You will see that you have the power, in each and every minute, to choose your thoughts and how you react to situations. Doing this will get you closer and closer to your purpose. As you lean into loving feelings, your path will become clear. You don't have to know the answers, you just have to have faith that they will appear.

And they will.

We get stuck in the thinking that we have to have it all figured out but that couldn't be further from how it actually works. It's not your fault, we've been conditioned to think ahead and plan. Sometimes that works to our benefit, especially back in the day when we'd have to outwit wild animals to survive but usually, in this day and age, we don't need to do that quite so much.

Make a commitment to your Intuition that you will start giving it the proper attention it deserves. Your feelings are how your Intuition communicates with you so start taking note. Take a moment before reacting and decide which reaction is one moving toward love and do that instead of reacting from a place of ego.

The more you connect to your Intuition, the more your purpose will come to the surface, so don't rush it. It's the journey--not the destination--that is important.

There are many ways you can begin to uncover your purpose by connecting to your Intuition. The key is to find things that work for you. You don't need to follow any rules because there aren't any. You do you.

Some ways I love to connect more deeply to myself are through:

Ritual— I love incorporating ritual into my daily life. You can also call this a daily practice. This could include anything from this list in any order, in any way. Make it your own!

Meditation— I love either setting a timer and focusing on my breath until my mind calms or listening to guided meditations such as those in the Yoga Goddess Academy membership or on the free Insight Timer app for iOS.

Creating a sacred space— I like to refresh my sacred space often to keep me inspired to do my practice. This space could include an altar as extravagant or minimal as you like. It could be one crystal and one picture of a holy person, for example. It could be more elaborate including a statue, a picture, a couple crystals, a small bottle of an essential oil, some fresh flowers, and a deck of oracle cards. It could even just be a yoga mat!

Using oracle cards— this is one of my favorite ways to really start listening to how your Intuition communicates with you. This will be different for all of us so this is an amazing way to tune into your Intuition's particular signs and feelings. I like to shuffle the cards while thinking of my question, which is usually something simple like, "Angels, spirit guides, and ancestors, please show me what I need to know today," but it could be more specific. Then I spread the cards out in two rows, rub my hands together and slowly move my right hand over the cards while holding the left hand open, facing the cards. I move my hand until I either feel a tingle in one finger of one my hands or until I just "feel" it's the one to draw. There is no right or wrong. Whichever card you pick, it is the right one. Practice having faith with this exercise.

Yoga— I practice asana (physical poses) to keep my body healthy but it's more than just physical health--it's mental and emotional as well. I love moving my body to release energy that is no longer needed and to explore where I may be holding on to old "stuff" or "stuck" energy.

Journaling— This is a great way to work through things that are bothering you or making you feel stuck. Write about what's happening in your life, things you've learned by not reacting, how you are growing spiritually, etc. Just by writing, you will tap into your innermost thoughts and feelings and your Intuition will use it as a form of communication.

Visualization— There's nothing I love more than daydreaming. I've been doing this since I was a child and I have a great imagination because of it. Let your mind soar. Dream about your ideal life, without damning the life you have now! Feel gratitude for those things that you KNOW are coming. Yes, this is a practice so you might as well start now! It gets easier with time.

Free writing— This is a bit different from journaling as you are just free-flowing with your words. Just start somewhere and let it go! Try to write two to three pages. This is a great way to tap into the deeper parts of your mind and subconscious and, of course, your Intuition!

Spending time in nature— Walking in nature is lovely! Unplug and focus on the scents, sounds, sights, and feelings around you. You can also bring any of these other practices outside!

Disconnecting from social media— Give yourself time to just be with yourself and those you love. Set a time each night to put your phone away and only check social media at certain points throughout your day. Turn off your notifications so you don't get tempted to check every five minutes!

Really enjoying the present moment by being grateful— Start appreciating the small things. Start by doing it while spending time with your children, pets, other family, or friends. Notice their amazing qualities or the awesomeness of the moment. Be grateful for being alive so you're able to enjoy the experience!

Moving my body in new ways— You can tap into your

Intuition by getting comfortable with letting your body move however it wants to. Start by turning on some sensual or mystical music and let your hips begin to move however it feels good. If you're not sure how, just start doing circles with your body—your knees, hips, shoulders, ribcage, and head!

Baths— Move your meditation to the bathtub! And as the water drains, visualize anything you no longer need to be rinsed away by the water that's going down the drain.

Using crystals— There is so much to learn about crystals and their benefits but you can also start building a relationship with them by just using the ones that you gravitate toward. You'd be surprised how many times I've picked up a crystal because I just "liked" it, then when I got home, I looked up the meaning and it was something that I was working on or needed to work on within myself!

Using essential oils— Same as above!

Taking a moment to process before reacting— In general, S L O W   D O W N. Pause. Take a minute. There's no need to rush, especially in difficult situations. Tune into your TRUE feelings instead of your Ego, who is always the first to react. Give others the benefit of the doubt. Realize we're all human. We're all doing the best we can with what we have. Don't worry about how others behave. It's not the situation but how you react to it.

Choosing Happiness

One of the practices that helps me stay in alignment the most is choosing happiness. Have you ever thought that being happy is a choice? There are people in the world with far less than you, yet, they're happy. There are people who have been through terrible experiences, and yet, they're happy. How can this be?

We all have the choice in every minute of every day to *choose* happiness. Something spill on your shirt right after you put it on? Fuck it, choose happiness. Did you stub your toe when you got out of bed? Fuck it, choose happiness. Did you get into a fender bender? Fuck that, too, choose happiness.

Sure, some things will be easier to get over and remain on the path of happiness but as long as you know it's all up to you then you have more *responsibility* to make that choice instead of playing the blame game. When it comes down to it, will the outcome of a shitty situation be a better one because you chose to be unhappy and pissed off about it? Definitely not. But it could potentially come out *way* better if you choose to remain happy.

It's not the experiences that define us, it's how we choose to react to them. It's not other people, situations, or the cards we were dealt that hold the key to a good life--it's how you choose to live despite them.

Ritual

Ritual is your daily practice and also any practices you do to connect yourself more fully to the natural rhythms of your body, the Earth, and moon, to name a few. It is a way for you to stay connected to Source, to stay tapped in and in alignment on a day-to-day basis. Going to yoga classes is great but it's super important to tune in daily so you can really deepen your personal connection to your

Inner Guru.

There is a difference between activities that "raise our vibration" and those that quiet the mind. Both can help you tap into your Intuition so it's important to do both. I do activities to "get into my happy place" whenever I need a pick-me-up. When you start paying attention to your emotions and realizing that they are just indicators of whether you're in alignment, you will then know that you can take a moment to "reset" and change the course of how your day will go. Just because you wake up on the wrong side of the bed doesn't mean that the rest of your day has to be terrible.

Some of these activities include:

- Reading spiritual books
- Gratitude writing
- Dancing to your favorite songs
- Singing your favorite songs
- Listening to spiritual audio recordings
- Praying
- Visualizing your dream life

But we need to make sure to QUIET the mind so that we can HEAR Spirit. Some of the ways we can do this are:

- Oracle cards
- Chanting
- Repeating a mantra
- Meditating
- Journaling

- Automatic writing
- Intuitive dancing
- Coloring
- Automatic/intuitive drawing

Sample Daily Ritual

- 10–20-minute meditation upon waking and BEFORE social media
- Gratitude journaling
- Spiritual lecture on YouTube, online membership, or online course
- Hanuman Chalisa practice
- 10–60-minute yoga practice

Some ways to incorporate more ritual into your life as a Goddess follow in the next few chapters.

CHAPTER 14

Creating Sacred Space

Sacred space is so important because it holds the energy of your intention and past meditations/rituals, gives you a focal point/center which will deepen your rituals, will encourage you to do your ritual, remind you of your intention, to stay aligned, or of your purpose throughout your day.

You can create your sacred space on a small side table, crate, windowsill, low dresser, a chair, or even in a box that you can move to wherever you have privacy.

You can decorate your altar with meaningful things from around your house, there's no need to go out and purchase a lot of new things. They should be things that inspire you, uplift you, connect you to your faith, help you feel aligned with Source, etc.

Seasonal items will also work or items from nature such as fresh flowers, plants, feathers, shells, rocks, pretty fabrics, sage, palo santo, and more.

Make sure to keep your altar clean and tidy. Remove any dead plants or flowers.

Some of your items may include crystals, your mala, a picture of a holy person, a holy book, statues, and more! The sky is the limit really. This should be very personal to you. Don't overthink it or try to decorate it how you think you "should." This is how you can start using your Intuition!

Over the next week, collect things from around your house and start setting them all in a neat little pile until you're ready to decorate.

GODDESS ASSIGNMENT:

- Create your sacred space
- Come up with a list of things you're going to try for the first week
- Commit to at LEAST five minutes a day but 10–15 will have more impact
- Don't stress
- Trust yourself
- Take notes in your journal when any symbols, imagery,

or words/phrases come to you in your meditations or even your dreams

- Google them with "dream meaning" or "spirit animals" and see what meaning it has for you

- Be aware of signs throughout your day. Notice any repeated or unusual sightings of certain animals, situations, songs, or items (such as feathers or pennies). Take note of these things and practice automatic writing/journaling.

- *Optional: Share a picture of your #SacredSpace on Instagram or in the Yoga Goddess Collective Facebook group with the hashtag #YogaGoddessAcademy

CHAPTER 15

Moon Cycles and the Divine Feminine

Girl, let me tell you, some weird shit has been going on lately. It's as though my Spirit is just doing its own thing in here! Over the past few months, when I find out what to focus on during the full or new moon, depending on what sign it's in and such (I don't know shit about astrology, so don't quote me on anything regarding it), I realize that I've actually been working on it already!

For example, this past full moon that happened last night, I was looking up some information on it, so I'd know how to go about performing some sort of personal full moon ceremony, when I read that this specific moon was all about letting go of deep-seated fears and anxieties that you've been holding onto for a while and bringing in more unconditional love.

Mind. Blown.

I had unconsciously been working on these things already for the previous month leading up to the full moon. How do I know? Because I was put in situation after situation that challenged my beliefs around my ability to have unconditional love for ALL, not just the people it's easy to do so with. I've had health issues that require me to face my fears and go to the damn doctor and face my mortality. My character has been judged and I've had people around me fling their emotional goo all over me, which as we all know, is really just my own shit being mirrored right back to me but in a different way.

Why do I have to know all these things? It would be much easier to just take a backseat and blame and criticize others instead but then I remember that is not why I came here to this lifetime.

Dammit.

So, onward with the work I must go. Trudging through all this stuff, and for some reason, feeling the need to share all my fuck-ups along the way with women like you.

The moon cycles are a brilliant thing and one that I've just recently begun working with over the past year or two. I feel such a connection to her and her energy.

A general rule of thumb for working with her energy is that when it is a New Moon, she will continue getting bigger and bigger up until the Full Moon. You can set intentions that are like seeds being planted. During this waxing phase, as the moon grows, so will your intention. You harness the power of that "growing" energy to give momentum to what you desire. When the Full Moon comes, you'll want to look back at what you created during the past couple of weeks in the waxing phase, and be grateful for anything that has manifested. Don't just look at the surface. Some things that you ask for may come in totally different ways than you'd expect.

You asked for patience but didn't get it handed to you on a platter? Well, did you get a billion experiences that were opportunities for you to practice building patience? Did you listen to your Intuition and use them for the learning and growing experiences that they were or did you damn the Universe for bringing you yet more frustrating experiences?

On the evening of the Full Moon, she is at her fullest. Every night from here on out until the New Moon, she will be getting smaller and smaller. This is the perfect time to harness the waning energy of the moon to release what is no longer serving you.

You can get way more into this and what each moon means astrologically but if you want to make it easy, just do what you are feeling. You know me, I'm all about leaning into my Intuition and I think it's best, as a general rule for myself, to do what is coming up for me personally rather than what others tell me the moon is supposed to mean. I like to look at the meanings, though, and if it correlates to what I've been feeling, awesome, bonus, but if not, I go with what I know I need personally. Usually, it's got a pretty broad meaning anyway so you can always find a way to weave in your intentions with what that particular moon energy is good for.

Some activities you can add into your moon ceremonies might include:

- Meditation
- Yoga
- Visualization
- Journaling
- Free writing (let your inner guide take over and write whatever comes up!)
- Free drawing (same as above but draw whatever it's feeling!)
- Dancing
- Singing
- Chanting
- Working with healing crystals
- Smudging with sage or palo santo
- Using pure essential oils
- Creating a vision board
- Taking an Epsom salt bath
- Reading spiritual books
- Getting out in nature
- Gathering with other women
- Cooking a healthful meal and infusing intention
- Connecting intimately with a partner or yourself to give more energy to the intention
- Starting a dialogue with your spirit guides, angels, or ancestors
- Going on a shamanic journey
- And really anything you feel called to do!

Feminine Cycles

Since working with so many women over the past few years, I've found that our feminine cycles usually correlate to the moon cycles in one way or another so you might want to track both cycles for a few months and see how they coincide. I always have my "Goddess Flow" just before the full moon and ovulate with the new moon but many women I know are the opposite or don't fall into either category. There is no right or wrong, it's something very personal to you that will help you to better understand your natural physical, mental, and emotional rhythms. What if you're not menstruating anymore or are super irregular? No problem! Again, each woman is unique.

If you do still menstruate, honor your flow by allowing yourself to fully rest on the first day, if at all possible. I try to do no physical activity except maybe a super gentle seated or restorative yoga flow to help comfort my body. If a nice, slow walk in nature helps your body feel better, do that but stay away from exertion and strenuous activity.

Another way to honor yourself and your cycles is to notice when you feel tired, uninspired, or want to be a hermit. Do take that time to crawl into a "hole" and let yourself unplug and recharge. Self-care activities are huge here. Taking baths with essential oils, spending time in nature, staying away from work for a couple days--all these things can help you gain back the energy you've lost from pushing so hard. You can't always be going. You have to find balance between the yin and yang or you'll burn yourself out which will do no one any good!

During parts of the month, you'll feel super energized, inspired, and ready to change the world! Honor yourself by getting the biggest tasks done early on in the day so you have a sense of accomplishment that will help push you along effortlessly with the rest of your to-do list. The key is to keep your to-do list short, only the things that HAVE to be done get on the main list. Anything extra is like a cherry on top, good, but not vital.

GODDESS ASSIGNMENT:

- Chart your emotions, cravings, mental outlook, energy level, sex drive, and anything else you feel is relevant.
- Notice which moon phases the similarities fall under and start to look for patterns over the course of three or more months.

Seasons

Another way we can connect to our physicality is by being in tune with the seasons. This is really important because, as spiritual-seekers, sometimes we spend way too much time in the more "mystical" realms which can cause us to lose sight of the "real world." You did choose to come here to experience the material world, after all.

One way you can start to get in tune is to start eating seasonally. For example, don't eat strawberries in December! You can easily go online and search for what foods would be in season during what time of year depending on where you live. Go one step further and support a local farm by joining their CSA (Community Supported Agriculture) program. Most farms have you pay a certain amount up front then, each week, or biweekly, you get a box stuffed full of seasonal produce.

As the wife of a farmer and someone who lives on a farm, the seasons are something I experience deeply. I have learned to enjoy the early nights of winter and the rest it brings not only to me but to Mother Earth who worked so hard in bringing a bounty of nourishing foods to my family and our customers.

If you don't live on a farm, like myself, get outside once a day, even for a short bit! Bundle up, if needed, and take a walk around the block. Feel the sun on your skin and notice the difference in the air each day. Where is the sun in the sky? How does the air smell? Is there moisture in the air or is it dry? What plants and animals do you see and what are they doing? All these questions will help you connect more deeply with the seasons and nature which will help you to better understand and appreciate your place within the system.

CHAPTER 16

We're All Sisters

Most of us have a point in our lives where we learned not to trust other women. It could have been learned from other women in your family or maybe you learned not to trust the women IN your family. For others, it was during puberty when some girls started looking more like women while others, who still looked like little girls, envied their womanly looks and the attention they got from the boys.

The thing is, those girls probably envied the slower growing girls because they weren't ready to handle everything that came along with looking like a woman. Perhaps it was in high school or college when you began competing with other women either in sports or academia or having the best clothes or being the skinniest.

Where does this need for competition with other women come from?

I read a book about a year or so ago by Lisa Lister in which she speaks of how women today have a great deal of mistrust of other women and it can, at least partially, be traced back to the witch trials. Women were pitted against each other out of fear for their own life. Can you imagine what it must have been like to live during that time? Even men weren't safe. Fear ran rampant and destroyed and ended countless lives and not even just in the United States. This has been happening for centuries.

We have to end the cycle now. We have to see that when we judge other women, compare and compete, or have jealousy toward them, it all stems from an insecurity within us. We have to be brave enough to face those emotions rather than burying them and continuing this vicious cycle. This is a cycle that can end now, don't teach it to your daughters. Don't bash other women with your friends.

Now is the time. Are you strong enough to handle it?

To be a pioneer of this movement all you need is a willingness to change. A willingness to put your TRUE self out there and be vulnerable because you know that while you aren't perfect, no one is, you're just one of the people brave enough to own that fact. A willingness to speak up.

When you do this, you will step into the role of a leader. Don't let this scare you! You are not a Guru, you will not SAY you are a

Guru, so you won't have that pressure. To be a leader just means that you are willing to go first and to share that journey with other women. Those that are ready to do the work will start to come out of the shadows and will be drawn to you because of your beautiful, imperfect light.

This is an honor. It is not an easy role to be in. Women will come to you, they may turn on you, they will love you and they will leave you. This is ALL OKAY.

It isn't your job to do the work for others. It is your job, if you want it, to initiate it and put that spark in others, letting them know they CAN do it and it WILL be okay if they do. It's a safe time now on this planet--more than ever anyway--to speak our truth as women. We've been silenced long enough and it's time to rise. We have a deep inner knowing that it's time to bring the planet's masculine and feminine back into harmony.

You don't have to be a leader like me or anyone else. You can create shifts by shifting your inner world. No two paths will be the same. Not everyone wants to be out in the forefront. You can still commit to doing your part to bringing about this shift, just decide what that will look like for you. For now, it may be committing to a daily practice of meditation. Maybe it's stopping negative self-talk or bashing of other women. It could look like finding more patience for your children or spouse. Whatever it is, it isn't "less than" or "less important" than those who choose to write books or get up on stage and talk about it. It all adds up to huge results. I want to thank you now for the work you are about to do and I'll be there for you, rooting for you, every single step of the way. Whether you know me personally or not, know that I am in your corner.

Goddess Gatherings and Spiritual Sisterhood

In my past, I have not had the best experience with women. Through my earlier years in high school, I learned that most women were something to be scared of because they probably didn't like me and would do things to make others feel the same. Though this idea may have been true then, it's not something I needed to carry around for so long.

It's time for women, of all beliefs, to come together and unify under the one belief we do share--that our voices matter. We can all make the world a better place and how great would it be if we had the support of our sisters in doing so?

I never thought that I'd be the creator and leader of an online community for women. However, the women in these groups have shown me what it means to be a truly strong woman who is so confident in herself that she has no problem lifting other women up. This is what it looks like to embody the Goddess energy. We don't all have to think the same to support each other in strengthening our voice. Any voice that comes from love is one that needs to be shared. And voices that come from somewhere else? Well, they have their place, too. We need contrast in our world, or we can never appreciate the good that abounds.

How can you tap into your tribe today? Do you have one? If this book is resonating with you, I highly encourage you to join the free online community so you can start getting the support, encouragement, and tools you need to rise.

Don't be scared to share your message because you think

someone is already out there sharing something similar. Trust me, the world needs to hear exactly what *you* have to say in exactly the way *you* would say it. No one has had the exact same life as you, therefore, cannot have the same viewpoint. What they will say to change the world will be entirely different from how you say it.

You must tap into your own inner Guru and let her show you the way.

CHAPTER 17

Tap Into Your Energy

To begin getting in tune with your inner Guru, you'll have to start getting in tune with the energy that runs throughout your entire being. This energy can be accessed through yoga, meditation, breathing (or pranayama), mudras, and much more!

Working with our own energy is one of the ways we can begin to really initiate change and growth. Becoming familiar with the chakras is a more tangible method to start developing a relationship with your own personal energy.

Have you ever felt butterflies in your stomach or a fluttering in your heart? That was quite possibly you tuning in to the energy of the chakra in that area.

Chakras are energy centers where "little rivers" of energy--also known as nadis--intersect. There are seven main energy centers that run through the central channel of the body known as the Sushumna. There are many more, and lesser-known chakras, throughout the body but the seven major ones are what we'll be focusing on in this book.

The chakras are part of an energy system that has ancient roots. The ancient yogis honored this system and many of the practices I lay out in this book are inspired by the chakras and finding ways to balance them to bring our being back into balance and harmony. If they are out of balance, either overactive or underactive, physical, emotional, mental, or spiritual symptoms may arise.

We can use yoga, meditation, and even the food we eat, and more, to find this harmony within this energy system.

It's important to note that you must discover if you believe the chakra is overactive or underactive. You must then choose practices to either calm or fire it up to bring it into balance.

Seven Main Chakras

1. Root— foundation, stability, finances
2. Sacral— emotions, relationships, creativity
3. Solar Plexus— manifesting, personal power, willpower
4. Heart— ability to give and receive love, compassion, empathy
5. Throat— ability to communicate and listen effectively, ability to speak your truth
6. Third Eye— intuition, psychic abilities, insight
7. Crown— consciousness and connection to higher

realms, bliss, realization

Root Chakra

Many of us have issues with our root chakra. Our root chakras start forming from the time we are born and throughout our first seven years on the planet while all the other chakras begin to form as well. It is a time of us getting familiar with this lifetime. It is located at our perineum and its color is red.

Other names for the root chakra are Muladhara, first chakra, and "base" chakra.

Associations of the root chakra:

- Fears
- Survival
- Worries about our stability in this life (strong foundations, money, etc)
- Primal instincts
- Connection or lack of connection to Mother Earth
- Connection or lack of connection to our family
- Addictions

At this stage in my life, I am working through fears that have been deeply seated in my being. When I was only a little over the age of one, my father died suddenly and unexpectedly. I'm still not even sure of the extent of the wounds but am fairly certain this experience has contributed to my addictions and also how I tend to put a wall up around me and think that I can do everything on my own because that's what I learned through that experience.

I relied on my mother heavily for most of my life and still do to a great extent but feel so much more secure in myself and find support from my connection to Source. That acceptance and love that I had lost so early in life are re-emerging in a totally new way that isn't dependent on anyone. But this allows me the capacity to fully love without expectations.

Root Chakra Balancing Tools

- Eat a diet rich in root vegetables, whole grains, and protein
- Use sacred essential oils such as Sandalwood, Frankincense, and Myrrh
- Repeat a Ganesh mantra such as "Om Gam Ganapataye Namaha"
- Practice standing mountain pose, bridge, and malasana
- Wear or decorate your altar with the color red
- Meditate on the color red
- Work with red, brown, or black crystals

JOURNALING EXERCISES

- What ways of thinking did you inherit from your family that are or aren't serving you any longer?
- What beliefs do you hold about money that aren't serving you any longer?
- What do you have fears around?
- Do you feel secure and stable? Do you have a strong foundation?
- Do you have a good connection to Mother Earth? Do you feel grounded? What can you do to deepen that connection?

Sacral Chakra

The sacral chakra is the next chakra up from the root. It is located in the central channel of the pelvic bowl and its color is orange. It's also called the Svadhisthana or second chakra.

While we are working on our establishing our root chakra up until age seven, we are also working on each of the other chakras up until that age as well to some extent. Once we work on establishing them during those first seven years, we come back around to them to develop them further and separately from the root.

The sacral chakra forms during our second year of life when we start to develop emotions, creativity, and a stronger connection to our family. We then come back to this chakra during the years 8-14.

This is a time when children start to learn more about their sexuality and what it means to be a man or woman. They often have their first relationships during this time and come into puberty.

Associations of the Sacral Chakra:

- Creativity
- Relationships
- Sexuality
- Feminine energy
- Emotions

This chakra is where our Divine Feminine energy resides. When we can more fully step into who we are as women, the more power we can harness from this chakra. Over the past couple of years, I've been working tirelessly on getting in tune with my Divine Feminine energy. It's never been something that has interested me before as I grew up a tomboy. And being a girl who'd rather play out in the barn than play with dolls, I didn't think I could be feminine, too. Now I realize that you can be whatever kind of Goddess you want to be and there is no specific mold you must fit into. We all have the power to tap into the Feminine Divine that can be used to create and shape worlds.

Sacral Chakra Balancing Tools

- Eat a diet rich in citrus and juicy fruits such as the meat from fresh coconut
- Consume orange foods
- Use essential oils such as bergamot, orange, and neroli
- Repeat a mantra devoted to Shakti, the primal Divine Mother energy
- Practice hip opening yoga poses and flowing, intuitive movements
- Wear or decorate your altar with the color orange
- Meditate on the color orange
- Work with orange crystals

JOURNALING EXERCISES

- Are you a creative person?
- Are you in tune with your sexuality and sexual needs?
- Do you feel like you can "go with the flow" of life?
- Are you confident in who you are as a woman?

Solar Plexus Chakra

The solar plexus, or Manipura chakra, is located about four fingers up from the belly button and below the diaphragm. The color that represents this chakra is yellow. It begins to develop around the age of three when we start to realize more fully who we are compared to others. How we are individuals.

The solar plexus starts to develop even more between the ages of 15-21. This is when we really start to become individuals and establish our sense of independence and who we are as a unique soul. We really begin to see how we are unique and start to think about how we want our life to look depending on what we believe our purpose here on Earth is for our lifetime.

This chakra is associated with:

- Personal power
- Self-discipline
- Independence
- Sense of identity
- Sense of responsibility for your life
- Manifesting

This chakra is one of the very first ones I really felt energy in. I get fluttering in this area when I get really excited about an idea that I am working on manifesting. I believe we use this chakra to manifest, or bring into being, those dreams that we came up with in our sacral chakra since that chakra is our seat of creativity.

I love manifesting and, for the past 15 years at least, I've been working hard on learning all there is to know about it and about the Law of Attraction.

I've manifested a lot of things but some of the ones that stick out the most and that I consciously worked on are:

- Selling our condo when it was REALLY hard to sell
- Finding a way to realize our dream of organic farming
- Moving into a much nicer house on a beautiful farm
- Creating endless opportunities
- Leading retreats locally and abroad
- Creating a thriving community
- Creating three successful businesses
- Touching the lives of hundreds of people

You can harness the energy of a balanced solar plexus chakra to manifest your dream life as well as to transform that which no longer serves you. I like to think of it as getting stable and grounded in the root chakra, bringing that energy up into the sacral chakra where we create or dream up our goals, then utilize the solar plexus to manifest these dreams into reality.

Solar Plexus Chakra Balancing Tools

- Eat a diet full of yellow foods such as lentils, pumpkins, and squash
- Use essential oils such as Juniper, Tea Tree, and Ylang

Ylang
- Repeat a mantra devoted to Lakini
- Practice twists and ab-strengthening poses
- Wear or decorate your altar with the color yellow
- Meditate on the color yellow
- Work with yellow crystals

Heart Chakra

The heart chakra is located in the center of the chest. Its color is green and begins to form during the age of four, while the root continues to form. This chakra is also called the fourth chakra or the Anahata Chakra. We often begin to show more affection and love to those close to us and become more sociable as we enter new learning environments when this chakra begins forming.

Here, we connect the lower, more earth-based chakras, with the more ethereal or spiritual based chakras. This is where we can learn to understand our emotions, which are our guideposts, to let us know if we are in alignment--body, mind, and spirit.

Throughout the ages of 22-28, we develop the heart chakra even more since we often get into longer-term romantic relationships at this time. This is also the time for more self-love and appreciation to develop, and we start to think about what we really want to do in this world.

The heart chakra deals with:

- Ability to give and receive love
- Compassion
- Empathy
- Relationships
- Forgiveness
- Self-love

It's easy for you to say that you love yourself, but do you really? Every aspect of yourself and who you've been over the years? I can't believe I'm 37 and finally just now beginning to take this seriously.

I grew up in a small town where everyone knows everyone. After leaving this area for Chicago, then Los Angeles, I never thought I'd find my way back here, but here I am! Growing up where everyone knew your business it was easy to fall into the trap of caring what others thought. I never really thought I DID care because, in high school, I was so different from the other kids and wasn't afraid to show it. Looking back, I think that was a coping mechanism. If I couldn't fit in with the "popular crowd," then I'd show them that I didn't WANT to fit in.

But most kids want to fit in and when you have one of your own, you want to give them every advantage. I find that in a small town, some people won't like you because of what you've done in your past and what your beliefs are now. It's hard when this may limit options for your child but it's made me do some soul-searching, and I realized that if that's how the parents are, that's probably how their children will be so why do I care? It's something I've had to let go of and to realize that I am doing all this work to show my daughter that she can be everything she ever dreamed of and more. I'm doing everything that scares me shitless every day because I know that's what will make me grow.

Will this make me everyone's cup of tea? Definitely not.

This is not my purpose. My purpose is to inspire those who feel like they've been given up on, or maybe have given up on themselves, that they matter. They are loved. They ARE love. No one is more special than another, not even if they have a perfect track record or go to church every Sunday.

I'm learning lessons now as a parent that I wish I had learned long ago but I know that there are many layers of learning on each subject. Just when you think you've healed, you're smacked with another, deeper lesson that you have to come to grips with in order to move forward. At least now I know that through this process, I can teach my daughter as well as my students what I've learned in hopes that they can heal that part of them and move forward without as much pain.

The writing of this book has made me grow up and face the fears of what others may think, yes, but even more scary, my family. Maybe they WILL think I'm weird, or that I tend to overshare or make a fool of myself, and that's okay. This is part of my growth process and part of me learning how to step out into my new, older, fearless self. Growing older doesn't have to be all bad. We have to find the good and appreciate every stage of life, or we'll forever be unhappy. I'm SO ready to stop living small, in others' shadows, afraid of what the world might think.

Are you with me?

Back of the Heart Space

When we're going through these difficult experiences in our life, it's so easy to just play the victim, to blame others, or blame our past. It's so much more empowering to remember that we CHOSE this life so that we could learn exactly what we are having the chance to now.

The outcome is up to you. Are you going to take this as a learning experience or are you going to sit in the lower energetic levels of blame, resentment, and unforgiveness?

I look at it like this. These experiences are hard and I know, because of my own history, that experiences JUST like this one will keep coming back over and over until I finally show up, accept it, and decide to learn and grow from it. The situations and people may change but the qualities of the struggle will be very similar so you can grow in the ways your Soul knows it must.

As a yoga teacher and spiritual guide, this can be a very difficult process to have those around you go through. When people aren't ready to look at their own shit, guess where it goes? Onto the easiest target, which is usually someone who is putting themselves out there, such as a teacher. This isn't fun to take the brunt of someone's shadows; however, this is one of the lessons that I have to learn in this life and that is to not take everything so personally!

I didn't put the pieces together but just remembered that I chose the intention this year to open up, look at, and release shadows from the back of my heart space. Wow! What a revelation. No wonder all these experiences are coming up!

To me, the back of the heart space has to do with:

- Obligations
- Devotion
- Feelings of "should"
- Deep feelings of self-acceptance
- Deep and utter forgiveness
- Total unconditional love
- Expectations of yourself and others
- Deep-seated anger, jealousy, and fear

I'm learning that it's easy enough to say that you love others and yourself, accept others and yourself and forgive, but I'm also learning that there are a LOT of layers to this process of learning and releasing our shadows. Just when I think I've learned to love others unconditionally, I have an issue with the ONE person who challenges me the most to see past our differences and send love and light to them anyway.

This is NOT easy and it's not really fun. But I do realize now that it's just what I asked for and I know that if I don't learn from it, something, probably worse, will come along to teach me the same exact lesson.

I feel the back of the heart space is where we go when we're ready to really look at the ugly stuff, the super painful stuff that we've swept under the rug because we wanted to forget. The stuff that was so painful or such a survival response that we didn't even realize we swept it under there. It's like cleaning out our basement.

The darkest, least-seen place in our home.

JOURNALING EXERCISES

- Who do I need to forgive?
- Do I need to forgive myself?
- Who is it hardest for me to truly love?
- Who am I holding resentment toward?
- What fears am I holding onto, especially when it comes to giving and receiving love?

Heart Chakra Balancing Tools

- Eat green, whole foods such as herbs, superfoods, green fruits, and green vegetables
- Use essential oils such as melissa, rose, and jasmine
- Repeat a mantra or sing a chant devoted to Krishna
- Practice heart-opening and upper back-opening poses such as puppy dog pose and camel
- Wear or decorate your altar with the color green
- Meditate on the color green
- Work with green or pink crystals

Throat Chakra

The fifth chakra is located in the center of the throat. Its color is blue and begins to develop around the age of five. Another name for it is the Vishuddha Chakra. At this time, we are learning how to express ourselves as well as how to find a balance with talking and listening.

The chakra develops further between the ages of 29-35. This is the time when we become more comfortable with who we really are as individuals and begin to speak our truth more fully. A lot of people really hone in on what their life's purpose is in this time period and may start making changes in their life to accommodate this purpose and path.

The throat chakra is associated with:

- Finding your purpose
- Speaking your truth
- Listening to others
- Confidence in speaking
- Connection to Intuition

Many people have imbalances in this chakra and they may show up as:

- Having a quiet, soft voice
- Getting sore throats often
- Not having a connection to their purpose

- Talking too much
- Not being able to fully listen to others
- Issues with their mouth including the tongue and jaw
- Telling lies

As I am just moving out of this stage and onto the next, I realize just how much I have been working on this chakra over the past few years. I have really begun finding a deeper purpose with my life and stepping more fully onto my path.

For years, I had no idea what I really wanted to do with my life. I was interested in many things but never could find the one thing that I wanted to dedicate a lot of time to until I found yoga. Being a yoga teacher served me for years while I taught at studios and community centers, but after I actually owned a studio, I realized how that path wasn't for me--I needed to have a platform where I could have a bigger voice to connect to the people that really resonated with me and that I really resonated with as well. Somewhere deep down, I knew finding a support system would be imperative on this journey.

After I sold my studio, I really began focusing my efforts online and now have a large community of women in a Facebook group. I've grown really close to a lot of these women, and they are the ones that come to the retreats I lead as well as take my online yoga teacher training. If it weren't for these women who continually showed up and supported my efforts, I would have given up long ago. They are my rocks.

When you find a tribe that lifts you up, despite what you may see as your shortcomings, you get more and more confident in sharing who you truly are with the world. It is my dream that moving forward on this planet, more women find a community of soul sisters who will be there for each other in the good times and in the bad. Who will share stories of how they've dealt with similar situations, how they grew from them, and how they aren't defined by them anymore.

This is the new age and this will create massive shifts. If you haven't found your tribe yet, some good places to look are Facebook groups, in-person meetups, local health food stores, sports teams for adults, crafting groups, and more. This may be the time that you have to try something new so you can get out of your comfort zone and meet new, inspiring people that can help you move your life in the direction you want to go so you can have the confidence to share your voice more fully with others.

Throat Chakra Balancing Tools

- Eat a diet full of whole, purple/blue foods such as purple peppers, plums, purple grapes, and purple potatoes
- Use essential oils such as Sage, Frankincense, and Clove
- Repeat a mantra devoted to Sakini
- Practice poses for the neck and shoulders
- Wear or decorate your altar with the color blue
- Meditate on the color blue
- Work with blue crystals
- Chant, sing, use your voice!

Third Eye Chakra

The sixth chakra is located in the center of the forehead and is where the three main energy channels converge and rise to the crown chakra. These energy channels are called "nadis" which translates to "little rivers."

Its color is indigo or purple and begins to develop around the age of six. It is also called the Ajna Chakra. In this stage of development, we are learning how to better understand our own thoughts and express them more clearly to others.

Between the ages of 36-42, it is believed that we further develop this chakra naturally by getting more in tune with our intuition as well as processing all the information we've learned in our lifetime so that we can better use that information.

This is the chakra that so many yogis strive to "open." They want to be better able to "see" with their third eye. I have definitely felt the same way but realized that without balancing the lower chakras or really connecting to the earth, or this lifetime, it's super easy to become ungrounded and disconnected from reality.

You've probably seen people like this before that seem so out of touch that they are hard to communicate with. I'm not saying there is anything wrong with this, I just know that, for me, I want to experience life as a physical being because that's what I chose to come here to do. If I was just living in my sixth and seventh chakras, I might as well be in spirit form!

I find it's best to have a balance between the two. Have a foot in both worlds by balancing not only these higher chakras but the lower, more Earth-based, ones as well.

On the surface level, a balanced third eye can be associated with:

- Intuition
- Knowledge that you are the creator of your reality
- Vision
- Connection to wisdom
- Abundance of inspiration and creativity

Other signs your third eye is "open" could show up as the ability to:

- Connect with angels, spirit guides, ancestors
- Astral travel
- Communicate telepathically
- "Just know" when things will happen
- Feel the energy/vibrations of others

Imbalances in this chakra may show up as:

- Delusions
- Illusions
- Feeling stuck in your place in life
- No clarity
- Nightmares
- No vision or inspiration

- OCD
- Not being able to see alternate ways of doing things
- Rejection of spirituality
- Scared to succeed

While I have been working on this chakra, unknowingly, for most of my life, it is now coming from a more grounded place with a broader perspective. This is the place from which I am able to help other women find their purpose and start moving toward their dream life. If you don't have faith or vision, it is nearly impossible to live the life you are meant to live.

Third Eye Balancing Tools

- Yoga inversions such as headstand, headstand, and shoulderstand
- Child's pose
- Wearing and surrounding yourself with purple or visualizing it
- Eating purple foods such as berries and plums
- Essential oils such as lavender, neroli, and frankincense
- Repeat a mantra dedicated to Shiva or Shakti
- Work with indigo or purple crystals
- Meditate, meditate, meditate!

The third eye is also heavily associated with the pineal gland. For centuries, this gland has been thought to hold the key to the unseen realms. Its name actually comes from the word "pine" because it is shaped like a pine cone.

When your pineal gland is calcified, or underactive from environmental causes, your third eye has a much harder time "opening" because, some believe, it depends on this gland for its vision and connection to higher states of consciousness. So, to find balance in your ajna chakra, begin working on decalcifying your pineal gland.

Tools to Decalcify Your Pineal Gland

- Stay away from fluoride, chlorine, and bromide
- Omit calcium supplements unless they have an equal amount of magnesium
- Avoid mercury and detox it from the body by taking chlorella, spirulina, and/or wheatgrass
- Eat organic fruits and vegetables
- Eat non-processed foods as much as possible
- Use natural beauty and skincare products
- Stay away from artificial sweeteners
- Look into the benefits of "skate liver oil" and consider taking it as a supplement

Crown Chakra

The seventh chakra, crown, or Sahasrara Chakra, is located at the crown of the head. It is represented by the colors white and violet and begins to develop around the age of seven. During this stage, we are completing the formation of the root chakra and beginning the work of the crown chakra. This is highlighted by our growing curiosity with the world at large and how we fit in it. We may begin to take more interest in spiritual concepts and how the world works.

The chakra develops further between the ages of 43 and 49. During these years, we may start to think more about death and our own spirituality. We may search for answers and have a thirst for knowledge. This can also show up as a "mid-life" crisis, but if handled properly, can actually result in massive growth, transformation, and understanding.

The balanced crown chakra may look like:

- A deep connection to spirituality
- An inner "knowing"
- A sense of being part of the whole
- Understanding and acceptance of death
- Sense of purpose

Imbalances in this chakra may show up as:

- Depression

- A mid-life crisis
- Skeletal problems
- Loss of identity
- Lack of purpose
- Sensitivity to light or sound

Crown Chakra Balancing Tools

- Fasting and detoxing both with food, social media, work, or addictions
- Eating nourishing foods
- Focusing on spirituality
- Meditation
- Use crystals such as selenite, clear quartz, and Amethyst
- Use essential oils such as frankincense, sandalwood, and vetiver

I feel that I've been in this stage over the past couple of years. While I am younger than the average age set forth here, I think we go through these stages when we are ready for them spiritually.

I believe I've been called to experience it earlier so that I can help others go through the process with more grace and ease.

I've seen many people really lash out during this time because they are lost and don't have the same sense of identity that they had in their younger years. It is truly a stage for transforming from the old you into a new, more mature soul.

If you find yourself in a mid-life crisis:

- Find a supportive friend or community that can help lift you up during this time
- Refrain from making big, life-altering changes
- Wait it out
- Find gratitude every day for what you *do* have
- Meditate . . . More
- Breathe deeply
- Get help if needed

CHAPTER 18

Dealing with Ascension

Ascension literally means "to rise" but in spiritual circles often refers to the process of going through a spiritual awakening or heading toward enlightenment. During this time, usually on and off on your spiritual journey, you may have symptoms show up that are hard to explain and hard to manage unless you know the spiritual, emotional, or mental cause.

It's my belief that these things need to be dealt with in order for you to grow, so symptoms flare up to give you a sign of what is out of balance and need your attention. The body really is a magical thing, and if you listen to it and develop a loving relationship with it, it will help you uncover what needs to be healed deep within your being.

One of the first symptoms I got from going through this process were flu-like symptoms. They came out of nowhere and my Intuition told me that it wasn't the flu. I listened to it, because that's what I do, and spent more time nurturing my body and soul with long baths, drinking a lot of water, and meditation.

Another one I get often is heart palpitations. When I am going through an energetic shift or feel like I'm receiving information, I'll get them. I used to get freaked out about them but, after going to the doctor and being told there isn't anything wrong with me, I relax, slow down, breathe, and allow myself to receive the new information. So I'm not saying don't go to the doctor when you're sick, but I am saying to tune in to your inner self and see what it has to say as well!

If you are reading this book, chances are you are already experiencing some symptoms, too. Some ways it can show up are:

- Flu-like symptoms
- Ringing in the ears
- Changes in vision such as "seeing things" like orbs, shadows, or sparks of light
- Heart palpitations
- Headaches
- Increased sensitivity to smell, light, and sound
- Chemical sensitivities
- Muscle spasms
- Increased electrical charge in the body

- More and more "synchronicities"
- Fatigue
- More need for alone time
- Increased telepathy
- Intense dreams

Watch for any new symptoms that may arise. When they do, tune in to your own inner Guru and see what comes up.

Notice what chakra they may correlate with, maybe you have work to do there. As needed, consult your physician, but keep in mind that your body is an extraordinary machine that is capable of bringing you messages to help you heal.

Knowing that you aren't alone will help you deal with these symptoms as well. When you know you aren't crazy, you can more effectively go within to uncover the causes.

Remember to reach out to your tribe of sisters and get support. You don't have to go through this alone.

CHAPTER 19

How to Keep the Inspired Momentum Going

Now that you have the tools, it's important not to put this book down and forget about everything you have uncovered and decided that you need to do in order to become the fullest expression of yourself. Your mission is way too important for that.

Yes, there may be challenges, but now you know that they are only there to help you grow. You have a different perspective that makes you grateful for the learning experience rather than mad about it "making your life harder."

You have to remember that you asked for it and if you didn't *consciously* ask for it, your Spirit did and it knows what's best for you and your journey.

Now, dear Goddess, it's time to get serious. It's time to get out there and change the world. Stay inspired and keep the momentum going by:

- Connecting with a tribe of sisters who will motivate you to do more, encourage you, and lift you up when times get tough.
- Coming up with a daily practice that works for you and stick to it, at least every weekday.
- Resting and taking care of YOU.
- Not blaming others and situations.
- Surrounding yourself with positive people.
- Doing the work to get to the root of the issues. Looking them straight in the eyes and dealing with them.
- Not judging, comparing, and thinking perfection exists.
- Choosing happiness and gratitude.
- Understanding that you have unlimited potential and can have everything you desire in your life.
- Having faith.

I know you can do this. You wouldn't have been called to read this book if you couldn't. You've read where I've been and how FAR down that was. You see that I've pulled myself out of it. You see what I learned from those experiences. If it weren't for those, I wouldn't be the person I am today. I wouldn't have the *mission* that I have today. If I can do it, trust me, you can, too. You can find your voice and your purpose and you can develop the confidence to share it.

All you need to do is . . .

Begin.

About the Author

Crystal Gray is an international yoga teacher who who is passionate about helping women step into their confidence, embrace their inner goddess, and create the life of their dreams.

Through Intuitive Flow Yoga Teacher Trainings, life and spiritual coaching, and beginner yoga programs, Crystal helps women show up where they're at and shine brighter than ever before.

When Crystal isn't guiding goddesses, she is a Mom, and she co-owns an organic vegetable farm in rural Illinois with her husband Marty.

To connect with Crystal on a regular basis, go to her website.

www.yogagoddessacademy.com

Acknowledgements

Where do I start? How do I even come close to thanking everyone who has had an impact in my life that has led me to where I am today and, therefore, what has came through in this book?

I guess all I can do is try my best.

I first have to thank my mom - my rock. She has gone through so much heartache in her lifetime and, still, has been there for me through all my craziness. She supports everyone who needs it and has been a shining example of how to be a great mom and a great person. Thank you.

To my family, without you, I wouldn't be who I am today. You've shaped me and I will forever love you all. Thank you.

Thank you to my daughter who, everyday, makes me want to be a better person. To my husband for letting me chase my dreams and giving me the freedom and opportunity to do so and for growing so much with me over this last decade - thank you. My love for you both grows stronger with each passing moment.

I have to thank my Goddess tribe. My loyal friends who I met through social media. Who could have dreamed that relationships like these could have started from a Facebook group? Without you, I would have never had the courage to bare my soul to the world. It is your loving encouragement that has given me the strength to do what I once thought was impossible. I love you for being open and honest and for letting me know that by me sharing my story, I would, in turn, help so many others. Thank you. I am forever grateful to you for helping me grow into the woman I am today.

Now to thank my beautiful tech and operations Goddess, Ysmay Walsh. She's behind the scenes and, somehow, continues to make me look organized and put together. Not only have you helped me to create everything in my business but you've coached and supported me when I've needed it most. You always make the time for me and your belief in me has given me the confidence to keep doing what I'm doing despite my fears. I love you.

Thank you to my true friends, new and old, who probably know way more about me than they'd like to, yet, still love me unconditionally. I hope you know who you are. I am forever grateful for your friendship.

To all my yoga and spiritual teachers along the way, I am indebted to you for all you've done to help me become who I am. This goes for actual teachers but also everyone in my life who has helped me grow and evolve. You've pushed my limits, made me cry, lifted me up and taught me how to be a leader and teacher myself. Thank you.

Thank you to all my yoga students and yoga teacher trainees. You've given me the confidence in my ability to teach and this has been the biggest gift. Without you, I would never believe in myself as I do now. I love you and I love watching you all shine your light in the world.

And last, but not least, thank you to Source, God, the Goddess. Thank you to my dad, spirit guides, angels and ancestors. You have walked with me, invisibly, every step of the way, in my life and definitely while writing this book. Thank you for leading me on a path that opened me up to my religion - love. It is my guiding force every day. Without it, this book would have never been written.

Thank you so much for reading, Goddess! Please take a moment and leave a short review on Amazon. I would love to hear what you think.

I would love to invite you to join our community of Goddesses on Facebook: Facebook.com/groups/YogaGoddessCollective where we have free trainings, livestreams, and more.

Made in the USA
San Bernardino, CA
09 June 2019